Evolution

Fact or Fiction?

Other books in the Fact or Fiction? series:

Evolution

Fact or Fiction?

Bruce Thompson, *Book Editor*

Daniel Leone, *President*
Bonnie Szumski, *Publisher*
Scott Barbour, *Managing Editor*

OPPOSING
VIEWPOINTS®
SERIES

GREENHAVEN
PRESS®

THOMSON
⎯⎯⎯✶⎯⎯⎯™
GALE

San Diego • Detroit • New York • San Francisco • Cleveland
New Haven, Conn. • Waterville, Maine • London • Munich

Cover credit: © John Reader/Science Photo Library

Cover caption: This seventy-meter trail of hominid footprints fossilized in volcanic ash was found by Mary Leakey's expedition at Laetoli, Tanzania in 1978. It dates from 3.6 million years and shows that hominids had acquired the upright, bipedal, free-striding gait of modern man by this date.

LIBRARY OF CONGRESS CATALOGING-IN-PUBLICATION DATA

Evolution / Bruce Thompson, book editor
    p. cm. — (Fact or fiction?)
Includes bibliographical references and index.
ISBN 0-7377-1591-X (lib. : alk. paper) — ISBN 0-7377-1592-8 (pbk. : alk. paper)
    1. Evolution (Biology) I. Thompson, Bruce E.R., 1952– . II. Series: Fact or fiction? (Greenhaven Press)
QH366.2.E8457   2003
576.8—dc21

2002033364

Printed in the United States of America

Contents

Foreword

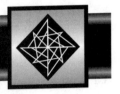

"There are more things in heaven and earth, Horatio, than are dreamt of in your philosophy."
—William Shakespeare, *Hamlet*

"Extraordinary claims require extraordinary evidence."
—Carl Sagan, *The Demon-Haunted World*

Almost every one of us has experienced something that we thought seemed mysterious and unexplainable. For example, have you ever known that someone was going to call you just before the phone rang? Or perhaps you have had a dream about something that later came true. Some people think these occurrences are signs of the paranormal. Others explain them as merely coincidence.

As the examples above show, mysteries of the paranormal ("beyond the normal") are common. For example, most towns have at least one place where inhabitants believe ghosts live. People report seeing strange lights in the sky that they believe are the spaceships of visitors from other planets. And scientists have been working for decades to discover the truth about sightings of mysterious creatures like Bigfoot and the Loch Ness monster.

There are also mysteries of magic and miracles. The two often share a connection. Many forms of magical belief are tied to religious belief. For example, many of the rituals and beliefs of the voodoo religion are viewed by outsiders as magical practices. These include such things as the alleged Haitian voodoo practice of turning people into zombies (the walking dead).

There are mysteries of history—events and places that have been recorded in history but that we still have questions about today. For example, was the great King Arthur a real king or merely a legend? How, exactly, were the pyramids built? Historians continue to seek the answers to these questions.

Then, of course, there are mysteries of science. One such mystery is how humanity began. Although most scientists agree that it was through the long, slow process of evolution, not all scientists agree that indisputable proof has been found.

Subjects like these are fascinating, in part because we do not know the whole truth about them. They are mysteries. And they are controversial—people hold very strong and opposing views about them.

How we go about sifting through information on such topics is the subject of every book in the Greenhaven Press series Fact or Fiction? Each anthology includes articles that present the main ideas favoring and challenging a given topic. The editor collects such material from a variety of sources, including scientific research, eyewitness accounts, and government reports. In addition, a final chapter gives readers tools to analyze the articles they read. With these tools, readers can sift through the information presented in the articles by applying the methods of hypothetical reasoning. Examining these topics in this way adds a unique aspect to the Fact or Fiction? series. Hypothetical reasoning can be applied to any topic to allow a reader to become more analytical about the material he or she encounters. While such reasoning may not solve the mystery of who is right or who is wrong, it can help the reader separate valid from invalid evidence relating to all topics and can be especially helpful in analyzing material where people disagree.

Introduction

Evolution means gradual change. Usually the word implies not just change but gradual improvement or progress as well. Nowadays the word is generally used to refer to a specific theory about life on Earth. According to this theory,

1. All (or nearly all) living things on earth are related to each other genealogically; in other words, life on earth forms a vast family, with a single common ancestor;

2. Life on earth has changed gradually from relatively simple forms to include relatively complex forms; and

3. This progressive change was caused by a natural process rather than being driven primarily by miraculous or supernatural intervention.

The question that this book considers is whether evolution is fact or fiction—that is, whether life on earth has evolved naturally from a relatively simple common ancestor to the complex forms that exist on earth today.

Evolutinists believe that life evolved accidentally from the comparative simplicity of nonlife. Creationists, on the other hand, hold that life was created intentionally by a higher intelligence capable of understanding and producing such complexity. The distinction between these two positions is not always clear-cut. Some creationists contend that life has gone through a process of progressive change, from simple to complex, guided by supernatural intervention. Some evolutionists maintain that an intelligent being exists, and created an initially simple universe, but then allowed that universe to develop according to its own laws into its present condition. Despite these exceptions, there is little room for middle ground between evolutionists and creationists, which is why opinion on this subject is so sharply divided.

Early Theories

Some ancient Greek philosophers, notably Empedocles, held the view that the universe could be explained entirely in terms of natural forces, without reference to an intelligent creator. Empedocles described the universe entirely in terms of elements and forces. He believed that the complexity of life emerged from a natural and accidental combination of four elements (air, earth, fire, and water) held in place by two forces (attraction, which he called "love," and repulsion, which he called "hate"). Empedocles believed that life began in the ocean and eventually developed the ability to survive on land—a view that now seems remarkably modern.

Most philosophers of that time, however, believed that life was too complex to emerge without help from some sort of preexisting intelligence. Indeed, most philosophers believed that the entire universe was a complex machine that was designed and built by a powerful deity. Their belief that the earth was at the center of the universe and that the planets moved in perfect circles around the earth probably contributed to this motion, since symmetry and regularity are characteristic features of machines. Aristotle, who lived soon after Empedocles, argued that the complexity of the world proved the existence of an intelligent designer. Aristotle's argument went virtually unchallenged for two thousand years. During the Middle Ages, it was even given a powerful restatement by St. Thomas Aquinas, who may have been the first philosopher to compare the universe to a clock. Clockwork was the height of technological achievement in the Middle Ages.

By the late eighteenth century, however, the idea of the "world machine" had begun to lose some of its appeal. It had been proven that the earth was not the center of the universe and that the planets did not move in perfect circles but in elliptical patterns that could only be described through mathematical approximations. The universe did not seem much like a machine after all, and the argument that the universe could have been produced only by an intelligent designer no longer felt convincing. The philosopher who expressed the skepticism of this period was David Hume, in his *Dialogues Concerning Natural Religion*. About the same time, the French biologist Jean-Baptiste Lamarck once again raised the possibility that life had emerged from the original simplicity of nonlife.

William Paley's Design Argument for the Existence of God

At the beginning of the nineteenth century, William Paley offered an argument to answer the skepticism of the late eighteenth century. Most people who read Paley's argument incorrectly assume that Paley was merely repeating the argument already given by Aristotle and Aquinas. This is not true. Paley understood that the old argument based on the idea of the "world machine" was no longer convincing. Moreover, Paley himself was not an astronomer or a physicist. By profession, Paley was an Anglican preacher, but he was also an avid naturalist, fond of collecting specimens of insects and plants in rural England. He was the first naturalist to observe how organisms are adapted to their environment, an idea that later became important to Charles Darwin. In fact, Darwin, who lived a generation after Paley, greatly admired Paley's work as a naturalist and even briefly took up the study of theology in an attempt to pattern his own life after Paley's.

Despite common misunderstandings, Paley's argument does not depend upon an analogy between a man-made machine (such as a watch) and the "world machine." Paley's argument turns solely on his observations of plants and animals, not on sweeping statements about the nature of the universe. Since Paley based his argument entirely on evidence drawn from biology and botany, it is appropriate to label Paley a "scientific creationist," although this is not a term Paley would have thought to apply to himself. Nevertheless, the arguments of modern creationists still follow the model set by Paley.

To see how Paley's argument differs from the older argument given by Aristotle and Aquinas, it is best to compare them side by side. Both the old argument and Paley's revision have two steps, but Paley reverses the order of the steps. It is an apparently simple change, but it has a dramatic effect on the strength of the argument. Read both arguments carefully.

It is immediately clear how weak the old design argument is. First, the argument by composition in the old argument is unconvincing. Argument by composition is an argument from parts to a whole, and in most cases it is not considered to be good reasoning. For example, all the old cars in a junkyard may be machines, but it does not follow that the junkyard itself is a machine. Similarly, even if it were true that most of the objects in the universe were machinelike, it would not follow that the entire universe was like a machine. The universe might just be a chaotic junkyard.

The argument by analogy is also weak. An argument by analogy is an argument in which similarities between two objects are used as evidence for further similarities. The more alike the two objects are, the better the argument is considered to be. For example, "Frogs are animals and hu-

Old Design Argument	Paley's Design Argument
Step 1: Argument by Composition	*Step 1: Argument by Analogy*
Observe the complexity of things in the world, including plants and animals. Since each of the parts of the world has the order and complexity of a machine, the whole world must be a machine.	Observe the complexity of plants and animals. They are all very similar to machines, like a watch. Since a watch is built by a prior being with intelligence, it is reasonable to conclude that each plant and animal is also built by a prior being with "intelligence" (namely its parents).
Step 2: Argument by Analogy	*Step 2: Argument by Composition*
Compare the world to a man-made machine, such as a watch. Both are machines. Since the watch was designed and built by an intelligent being, it is reasonable to conclude that the world was also designed and built by an intelligent being (namely God).	Since each plant and animal must be built by parents that are as complex, or as "intelligent," as it is, nature is found to be a long sequence of entities, each coming from and giving rise to further entities in the sequence. Since every *part* of the sequence is built by a prior intelligent being, the *whole* sequence must be built by a prior intelligent being (namely God).

mans are animals. Since humans feel pain, it is reasonable to conclude that frogs also feel pain." This seems to be a pretty convincing argument. But now consider, "Trees are alive and humans are alive. Since humans feel pain, it is reasonable to conclude that trees also feel pain." This argument does not sound at all convincing, since trees are not very similar to humans. Yet trees and humans clearly have more in common than watches and universes. Hence it should be obvious that an argument that compares the universe to a watch is too weak to be persuasive.

But now look at Paley's argument. Despite common misunderstandings, Paley does not compare his watch to the whole universe. He merely compares it to *living things*. The similarity between man-made machines and living organisms is extremely strong. It is because organisms are like machines that people can use the principles of physics and chemistry to understand how they work. Every scientist is willing to admit that living organisms are "machines" in the sense that Paley intends. Moreover, every scientist draws the same conclusion that Paley draws: Living things are complex because they grow from previously existing complex entities, their parents.

Paley's argument by composition is also a significant improvement. Some arguments by composition can be quite convincing. For example, look at the book you are now holding. This page is made of paper, and so are all of the other pages (as well as the cover and spine). Since each *part* of the book is made of paper, the book *as a whole* is made of paper. Paley's argument by composition seems more like this than like the junkyard argument considered previously. If each member (or part) of a sequence is "intelligent," and it derives its intelligence from the fact that it was built by a previous member of the sequence *with equal or greater intelligence*, then it is not wrong to conclude that the sequence *as a whole* has "intelligence," which it derived from a previously existing intelligent being. By "intelligence," Paley does not necessarily mean conscious knowledge. A mother does not consciously know how to grow a baby. Yet her body is encoded with the necessary information. The mother's body has the "intelligence" to construct the baby, even if the mother is not able to explain, or even comprehend, how the process works. But where could such intelligence have come from? It came from the body of the mother's mother, which came from the body of a mother before that, and so on. Ultimately, according to Paley's argument, it must have come from God.

Paley himself saw only one possible flaw in this argument. He recognized that, if it were possible for a long sequence of "intelligent" entities to become slightly more complex, or "intelligent," with each new generation, then it might be possible for the sequence to be traced back to an entity that was so simple that it might have fallen together merely by sheer accident: "If the difficulty [of producing complexity from simplicity] were diminished the farther we went back, by going back indefinitely we might exhaust it."[1] In other words, if life has become progressively more complex over time, then it may be possible to trace life back to a form so simple that it might have emerged by accident. Paley recognized that his argument was valid only as long as there was no conceivable natural process by which the complexity of living things could increase over time. However, Paley was not worried. In 1802, no one knew of any such process. Some thinkers, such as Lamarck, believed in evolution, but no one could explain how evolution could happen *naturally*—in other words, according only to physical laws without any sort of intelligent direction. Lamarck's theory of evolution, which appealed to a sort of internal "power of life," was no threat to Paley's argument.

William Paley's argument was a triumph. He quickly became one of the most celebrated English philosophers. His argument even sparked a school of thought in science known as the natural theology movement. As part of this movement, a popular series of books, known as the *Bridgewater Treatises*, were published in the first half of the nineteenth century to discuss what science could teach people about God. Some of the most respected and influential scientists of the day contributed to the *Bridgewater Treatises*.

The Theory of Natural Selection

The natural theology movement was short-lived. In 1858 two men jointly announced that they had discovered a process that could cause the complexity of organisms to increase by slow increments over long periods of time. These two men were Alfred Russel Wallace and Charles Darwin, and they called their process "natural selection."

Darwin and Wallace were about as different from each other as two men could be. Darwin was a shy man and a cautious thinker who did not relish controversy. Wallace was rather flamboyant and not afraid of controversy. Darwin was the first to discover the theory of natural selection. However, he knew that the theory would be controversial, so he proceeded to work on the idea privately for another twenty years, gathering evidence and mustering arguments. He wanted to make sure that, when the idea was finally presented, it would be backed up by such a massive body of evidence that it could not be dismissed. Only a few of Darwin's friends in the scientific community knew what he was working on.

When Wallace came up with the idea of natural selection in 1858, he immediately wrote a short paper explaining the idea and sent it to Darwin (who was already a respected naturalist) for his opinion. Wallace thought the idea was so clear and obvious that it would be accepted without needing masses of observational data. He was ready to publish. If either Darwin or Wallace had been an ambitious glory-seeker, the matter might have turned into an ugly dispute over who had the right to claim credit for the idea. However, both men were happy to share the credit. In July 1858, papers by Darwin and Wallace were presented jointly to a meeting of the Linnean Society. The theory of natural selection had been made available to the scientific community and to the world.

Of course, Darwin was right. The theory was very controversial, and the twenty years he spent carefully collecting data paid off. Within a few years, nearly every scientist had accepted the idea that evolution was a fact and that it could be explained by the process of natural selection. However, while Wallace's article was a brilliant piece of reasoning, it was Darwin's evidence that made the biggest impression. Today, Darwin's name is closely associated with the theory of natural selection. Very few people have heard of Alfred Russel Wallace.

Natural Selection Explained

It is important to understand that Darwin (and Wallace) did not merely propose the idea that life evolves. As has been discussed, that is an old idea that can be found even among the ancient Greeks. Prior to Darwin, Lamarck believed in evolution, and even Darwin's grandfather, Erasmus Darwin, believed in evolution. But no one could offer a convincing explanation of how evolution might work. What Darwin and Wallace did was not simply propose that life *evolves* but describe a naturalistic mechanism that could *cause* it to evolve.

The theory of natural selection involves three key concepts:
1. Replication
2. Competition
3. Open-ended variation

Replication occurs when one entity makes (or is used to make) copies of itself. Naturally, living things replicate, since each new generation of living organisms copies the characteristics of the previous generation. New organisms are copies of their parents.

Competition occurs when some factors limit how many copies can be made or how many copies are able to survive. Again, living organisms provide the clearest example. Organisms need food to survive, and the amount of available food is limited. Hence, some organisms are more successful than others at surviving and making copies of themselves.

Variations are slight "imperfections" in the copying process, so a new generation is not exactly like the parent generation in every respect. These variations must be minor. New entities must be enough like their parents to be considered copies. Variations that are too great will no longer preserve the characteristics of the parent generation and therefore will not count as copies. However, the variations must also be truly open-ended, not limited within fixed boundaries. It must be possible for genuinely new and unpredictable characteristics to arise. For example, suppose you copy a sequence of letters, making slight changes every time you copy the sequence. If the sequence is limited to only three letters, you might be able to produce a sequence like this: CAT . . . BAT . . . BAD . . . BED . . . RED . . . etc. You could continue in this manner for a while, but eventually you would run out of new combinations, and you could never produce words more complex than the one you began with. Now suppose that the number of letters was among the features you were allowed to vary. In this case, the variation would be open-ended, since genuinely new combinations would always be possible. For example, you could produce a sequence such as the following: A . . . AT . . . CAT . . . BAT . . . BIT . . . BITE . . . etc. As the process continues, more complex words could be formed from simpler words.

Whether living organisms are subject to such minor open-ended variations has been a controversial question. Creationists generally believed (and still believe) that life can vary only within fixed boundaries. Wallace argued that living organisms could vary in an open-ended manner; Darwin looked for (and found) evidence of surprisingly new, and therefore presumably open-ended, variations among artificially bred pigeons. However, without a knowledge of modern genetics, Darwin and Wallace could only guess that they were right. Now that scientists understand how DNA molecules operate, it has been proven that organisms are in fact subject to open-ended variation. Small errors in the copying of DNA molecules during meiosis (the process of producing egg and sperm cells) give rise to minor variations. Since the *length* of the DNA molecule, not just the sequence of amino acids that make it up, is subject to variation, the variation is open-ended, just as Darwin and Wallace had supposed it was.

Given these three basic factors—replication, competition, and open-ended variation—evolution seems almost necessary. Of the minor variations that occur in any generation, many may create offspring that are simpler than their parents; most will be neither simpler nor more complex; and a few will actually produce offspring that are (slightly) more complex than their parents. In some (but not all) cases, the complex offspring will also have an advantage in the competition to survive and reproduce, and will therefore produce many copies of themselves. Again, a few of these copies may be both more complex than their parents and better able to survive and reproduce than their siblings. As this process continues, slowly—but inexorably—complexity will tend to increase along at least *some* of the generational lines, although certainly not along all of them. The eventual result will be a wide variety of living organisms, ranging from extremely simple to quite complex, just as we observe in life on earth today.

The theory of natural selection per se does not explain the origin of life. The theory applies only to entities that replicate (with minor variations) and are in competition with each other. This is not an accurate description of most nonliving things. Hence, the theory of natural selection does not explain how life might have emerged from nonlife; it only explains how life *changes* (i.e., how new species emerge from older species) given that life already exists.

However, it is important to understand that the theory of natural selection does make it much easier to explain the origin of life. Assuming that the theory of natural selection is true, it is only necessary to explain the origin of the very simplest self-replicating entities. Thereafter, natural selection will cause more complex entities to emerge. These simplest of self-replicating entities may have been so simple that it is statistically possible for them to have occurred randomly, or by sheer accident, without any help from God.

Natural Selection Since Darwin

Since the theory of natural selection was first proposed, it has undergone some development, although the underlying concepts have not changed. The most important development was the synthesis of Darwinism with theories in genetics. Genetic theory was first worked out by a French monk named Gregor Mendel. This work was actually done while Darwin and Wallace were still alive; however, it was not widely known at the time, so neither Darwin nor Wallace was aware of it. It was not until the 1930s that evolutionists such as Theodosius Dobzhansky began to use genetics to explain the variation that natural selection requires. And it was not until the 1960s, when James Watson and Francis Crick proposed the double-helix structure of the DNA molecule, that the minor but open-ended errors in genetic copying (during meiosis) were fully understood.

During the 1970s, two evolutionists, Niles Eldridge and Stephen Jay Gould, stirred up controversy by proposing that evolution due to natural selection does not move at a slow, steady pace. They argued that the process of evolution tended to move relatively rapidly during periods of ecological stress (e.g., during climate changes or when continents came into contact with each other due to continental drift) but that most of the time natural selection did not produce much evolutionary change. They called their view "punctuated equilibrium." In his earlier writings, Gould occasionally characterized his theory of punctuated equilibrium as a significant departure from classical Darwinism.

Because of the controversy caused by the theory of punctuated equilibrium, opponents of evolution have sometimes tried to describe modern evolutionary theory as divided and chaotic. This is not true. Today the debate over punctuated equilibrium has largely been settled, and the new consensus appears to be this: Eldridge and Gould were right that the pace of evolution varies depending on how rapidly the environment itself is changing. However, they probably overstated their case in characterizing their theory as a departure from classical Darwinism. In fact, their view still appeals to exactly the same fundamental principles that have been part of Darwinism from the beginning—namely, replication, competition, and variation.

Opponents of evolution also sometimes charge that Darwinists are atheists and that the hidden agenda of Darwinism is to promote atheism. While some Darwinists are undoubtedly atheists, many are not. Many people believe that God created the basic structure of the universe—the fundamental laws of physics—knowing that this basic structure was capable of giving rise to complex life out of an initial chaos. Presumably, God even foresaw what direction the random processes he had created would take. Thus, many people are able to reconcile a belief in God with a belief in evolution.

Creationism Since Darwin

Meanwhile, the creationism of the nineteenth century has also undergone some development. When the theory of natural selection was first proposed, not all of the scientists who had been part of the natural theology movement were persuaded. However, even most creationists had already accepted the idea (based on geological evidence) that the earth was quite old and that the "days" of creation mentioned in the Bible were not to be taken as referring to periods of twenty-four hours. Many creationists believed that the "days" of creation represented long ages during which God had created (and in some cases, destroyed) many forms of life, beginning with the simpler forms and progressing toward humanity. According to this view, of course, separate forms of life were not related to each other genealogically. Having accepted the idea of an old earth, it was relatively easy for some creationists to accept the idea that much of life is genealogically related and that the more complex forms had developed from the simpler forms. However, creationists did not accept the idea that this progressive change was caused by natural selection. They preferred to believe that God was directing the process. Some creationists who accepted this view continued to insist that humanity came about through a special act of creation and that humans were not genealogically related to apes and other living things. William Jennings Bryan, for example, believed that progressive changes in life forms had taken place over vast eons since the earth's creation. However, he also believed that Adam and Eve had been created recently by God and had not been produced by evolution. Harry Rimmer, a creationist during the same period, also believed that the earth was very old and that the story of Noah's flood was folklore based on a local event.

The exception to this general acceptance of the old earth

was George McCready Price, who proposed interpreting the facts of geology, including the fossil record, as evidence for a literal worldwide flood, as described in the Bible. Like Darwin, Price spent twenty years gathering evidence and honing his arguments before publishing them in *The New Geology* in 1923. Price's arguments were dismissed by established geologists, but they did eventually come to be accepted among Christian fundamentalists. In 1961 his arguments were restated (with minor changes) by John Whitcomb and Henry Morris in their book *The Genesis Flood,* and in 1974 the textbook *Scientific Creationism* presented Price's flood geology as the scientific alternative to the old-earth geology accepted by Darwinists.

The modern term *scientific creationism* is generally used to refer to the view, espoused by Price and his more recent advocates, that evolution could not have taken place at all because the earth is too young for such a gradual process to have had any effect. According to this view, the facts of geology and biology have been misinterpreted by established scientists and should be correctly interpreted as validating the story of a worldwide flood. Just as Darwinists have moved toward consensus on a single theory, creationists have done the same. Nowadays the outspoken critics of evolution tend to endorse flood geology. Advocates of divinely guided progressive change have largely been converted either to true Darwinism or to young-earth creationism.

Because the young-earth version of creationism is so obviously based on a literal understanding of the Bible, opponents of creationism are inclined to describe the creationist movement as a pseudoscientific attempt to misuse the vocabulary of science to promote a religious agenda. During the first half of the twentieth century, this characterization was largely true. Among well-known advocates of young-earth creationism, none possessed earned scientific credentials, although some were eventually awarded honorary degrees by conservative Christian colleges. However, what may have been true then is no longer true. Ronald Numbers, who has chronicled the history of the creationist movement, describes the rise of modern creationism:

> Although scientifically trained creationists, especially in the biological and earth sciences, had become an endangered species by the early years of the [twentieth] century, they gradually reappeared as more and more fundamentalist youth sought higher education. . . . In 1963, when the Creation Research Society was organized, five of its ten founders held earned doctorates in biology from major universities, and two others possessed Ph.D.s in science or engineering.[2]

Today, there are more creationists, and more highly educated creationists, than ever. Clearly, the debate over whether evolution is fact or fiction is only just beginning.

Notes

1. William Paley, *Natural Theology: Evidences of the Existence and Attributes of the Deity.* Philadelphia: H. Maxwell, 1802.
2. Ronald L. Numbers, *The Creationists.* Berkeley: University of California Press, 1992, p. xiv.

Chapter 1

Fact or Fiction?

Evidence in Support of Creationism

The Natural World Provides Evidence of Design

William Paley

Can scientific evidence be used either to confirm or discon-
firm the existence of God? Darwinists feel that God has no
role in science, since science should try to find natural, not
supernatural, explanations for the phenomena they observe. Creationists, by contrast, believe that the natural
world provides clear evidence for the existence of a creator.
There is no more compelling statement of this position
than the one given by William Paley.

William Paley (1743–1805) was an Anglican theologian
and Archdeacon of Carlisle in rural England. He was an avid
naturalist, fond of collecting specimens.

The following selection is Paley's famous "design argument" for the existence of God, taken from his book *Natural
Theology*. The same argument, which draws an analogy between a man-made watch and the complex productions of
nature, is still used by modern creationists.

William Paley, *Natural Theology: Evidences of the Existence and Attributes of the
Deity*. H. Maxwell, 1802.

In crossing a heath, suppose I pitched my foot against a *stone* and were asked how the stone came to be there. I might possibly answer that for anything I knew to the contrary it had lain there forever; nor would it, perhaps, be very easy to show the absurdity of this answer. But suppose I had found a *watch* upon the ground, and it should be inquired how the watch happened to be in that place, I should hardly think of the answer which I had before given, that for anything I knew the watch might have always been there. Yet why should not this answer serve for the watch as well as for the stone; why is it not as admissible in the second case as in the first? For this reason, and for no other, namely, that when we come to inspect the watch, we perceive—what we could not discover in the stone—that its several parts are framed and put together for a purpose, e.g., that they are so formed and adjusted as to produce motion, and that motion so regulated as to point out the hour of the day; that if the different parts had been differently shaped from what they are, or placed after any other manner or in any other order than that in which they are placed, either no motion at all would have been carried on in the machine, or none which would have answered the use that is now served by it. To reckon up a few of the plainest of these parts and of their offices, all tending to one result: we see a cylindrical box containing a coiled elastic spring, which, by its endeavor to relax itself, turns round the box. We next observe a flexible chain—artificially wrought for the sake of flexure—communicating the action of the spring from the box to the fusee. We then find a series of wheels, the teeth of which catch in and apply to each other, conducting the motion from the fusee to the balance and from the balance to the pointer, and at the same time, by the size and shape of those wheels, so regulating that motion as to terminate in causing an index, by an equable and measured progression, to pass over a given space in a given time. We take notice that the wheels are made of brass, in order to keep them from rust; the springs of steel, no other metal being so elastic; that over the face of the watch there is placed a glass, a material employed in no other part of the work, but in the room of which, if there had been any other than a transparent substance, the hour could not be seen without opening the case. This mechanism being observed—it requires indeed an examination of the instrument, and perhaps some previous knowledge of the subject, to perceive and understand it; but being once, as we have said, observed and understood—the inference we think is inevitable, that the watch must have had a maker— that there must have existed, at some time and at some place or other, an artificer or artificers who formed it for the purpose which we find it actually to answer, who completely comprehended its construction and designed its use.

Replies to Critics

I. Nor would it, I apprehend, weaken the conclusion, that we had never seen a watch made—that we had never known an artist capable of making one—that we were altogether incapable of executing such a piece of workmanship ourselves, or of understanding in what manner it was performed; all this being no more than what is true of some exquisite remains of ancient art, of some lost arts, and, to the generality of mankind, of the more curious productions of modern manufacture. Does one man in a million know how oval frames are turned? Ignorance of this kind exalts our opinion of the unseen and unknown artist's skill, if he be unseen and unknown, but raises no doubt in our minds of the existence and agency of such an artist, at some former time and in some place or other. Nor can I perceive that it varies at all the inference, whether the question arise concerning a human agent or concerning an agent of a different species, or an agent possessing in some respects a different nature.

II. Neither, secondly, would it invalidate our conclusion, that the watch sometimes went wrong or that it seldom went exactly right. The purpose of the machinery, the design, and the designer might be evident, and in the case supposed, would be evident, in whatever way we accounted for the irregularity of the movement, or whether we could account for it or not. It is not necessary that a machine be perfect in order to show with what design it was made: still less necessary, where the only question is whether it were made with any design at all.

III. Nor, thirdly, would it bring any uncertainty into the argument, if there were a few parts of the watch, concerning which we could not discover or had not yet discovered in what manner they conduced to the general effect; or even some parts, concerning which we could not ascertain whether they conduced to that effect in any manner whatever. For, as to the first branch of the case, if by the loss, or disorder, or decay of the parts in question, the movement of the watch were found in fact to be stopped, or disturbed, or retarded, no doubt would remain in our minds as to the utility or intention of these parts, although we should be unable to investigate the manner according to which, or the connection by which, the ultimate effect depended upon their action or assistance; and the more complex the machine, the more likely is this obscurity to arise. Then, as to the second thing supposed, namely, that there were parts which might be spared without prejudice to the movement of the watch, and that we had proved this by experiment, these superfluous parts, even if we were completely assured that they were such, would not vacate the reasoning which we had instituted concerning other parts. The indication of contrivance remained, with respect to them, nearly as it was before.

IV. Nor, fourthly, would any man in his senses think the existence of the watch with its various machinery accounted for, by being told that it was one out of possible combinations of material forms; that whatever he had found in the place where he found the watch, must have contained some internal configuration or other; and that this configuration might be the structure now exhibited, namely, of the works of a watch, as well as a different structure.

V. Nor, fifthly, would it yield his inquiry more satisfaction, to be answered that there existed in things a principle of order, which had disposed the parts of the watch into their present form and situation. He never knew a watch made by the principle of order; nor can he even form to himself an idea of what is meant by a principle of order distinct from the intelligence of the watchmaker.

VI. Sixthly, he would be surprised to hear that the mechanism of the watch was no proof of contrivance, only a motive to induce the mind to think so:

VII. And not less surprised to be informed that the watch in his hand was nothing more than the result of the laws of *metallic* nature. It is a perversion of language to assign any law as the efficient, operative cause of any thing. A law presupposes an agent, for it is only the mode according to which an agent proceeds: it implies a power, for it is the order according to which that power acts. Without this agent, without this power, which are both distinct from itself, the *law* does nothing, is nothing. The expression, "the law of metallic nature," may sound strange and harsh to a philosophic ear; but it seems quite as justifiable as some others which are more familiar to him, such as "the law of vegetable nature," "the law of animal nature," or, indeed, as "the law of nature" in general, when assigned as the cause of phenomena, in exclusion of agency and power, or when it is substituted into the place of these.

VIII. Neither, lastly, would our observer be driven out of his conclusion or from his confidence in its truth by being told that he knew nothing at all about the matter. He knows enough for his argument; he knows the utility of the end; he knows the subserviency and adaptation of the means to the end. These points being known, his ignorance of other points, his doubts concerning other points affect not the certainty of his reasoning. The consciousness of knowing little need not beget a distrust of that which he does know.

A Watch That Can Reproduce

Suppose, in the next place, that the person who found the watch should after some time discover that, in addition to all the properties which he had hitherto observed in it, it possessed the unexpected property of producing in the course of its movement another watch like itself—the thing is conceivable; that it contained within it a mechanism, a system of parts—a mold, for instance, or a complex adjustment of lathes, files, and other tools—evidently and separately calculated for this purpose; let us inquire what effect ought such a discovery to have upon his former conclusion.

I. The first effect would be to increase his admiration of the contrivance, and his conviction of the consummate skill of the contriver. Whether he regarded the object of the contrivance, the distinct apparatus, the intricate, yet in many parts intelligible mechanism by which it was carried on, he would perceive in this new observation nothing but an additional reason for doing what he had already done—for referring the construction of the watch to design and to supreme art. If that construction *without* this property, or, which is the same thing, before this property had been noticed, proved intention and art to have been employed about it, still more strong would the proof appear when he came to the knowledge of this further property, the crown and perfection of all the rest.

II. He would reflect that, though the watch before him were *in some sense* the maker of the watch which was fabricated in the course of its movements, yet it was in a very different sense from that in which a carpenter, for instance, is the maker of a chair—the author of its contrivance, the cause of the relation of its parts to their use. With respect to these, the first watch was no cause at all to the second; in no such sense as this was it the author of the constitution and order, either of the parts which the new watch contained, or of the parts by the aid and instrumentality of which it was produced. We might possibly say, but with great latitude of expression, that a stream of water ground corn; but no latitude of expression would allow us to say, no stretch of conjecture could lead us to think that the stream of water built the mill, though it were too ancient for us to know who the builder was. What the stream of water does in the affair is neither more nor less than this: by the application of an unintelligent impulse to a mechanism previously arranged, arranged independently of it and arranged by intelligence, an effect is produced, namely, the corn is ground. But the effect results from the arrangement. The force of the stream cannot be said to be the cause or the author of the effect, still less of the arrangement. Understanding and plan in the formation of the mill were not the less necessary for any share which the water has in grinding the corn; yet is this share the same as that which the watch would have contributed to the production of the new watch, upon the supposition assumed in the last section. Therefore,

III. Though it be now no longer probable that the individual watch which our observer had found was made immediately by the hand of an artificer, yet this alteration does not in anywise affect the inference that an artificer had been originally employed and concerned in the production. The argument from design remains as it was. Marks of design and contrivance are no more accounted for now than they were before. In the same thing, we may ask for the cause of different properties. We may ask for the cause of the color of a body, of its hardness, of its heat; and these causes may be all different. We are now asking for the cause of that subserviency to a use, that relation to an end, which we have remarked in the watch before us. No answer is given to this question by telling us that a preceding watch produced it. There cannot be design without a designer; contrivance without a contriver; order without choice; arrangement without anything capable of arranging; subserviency and relation to a purpose without that which could intend a purpose; means suitable to an end, and executing their office in accomplishing that end, without the end ever having been contemplated or the means accommodated to it. Arrangement, disposition of parts, subserviency of means to an end, relation of instruments to a use imply the presence of intelligence and mind. No one, therefore, can rationally believe that the insensible, inanimate watch, from which the watch before us issued, was the proper cause of the mechanism we so much admire in it—could be truly said to have constructed the instrument, disposed its parts, assigned their office, determined their order, action, and mutual dependency, combined their several motions into one result, and that also a result connected with the utilities of other beings. All these properties, therefore, are as much unaccounted for as they were before.

A Series of Contrivances

IV. Nor is anything gained by running the difficulty farther back, that is, by supposing the watch before us to have been produced from another watch, that from a former, and so on indefinitely. Our going back ever so far brings us no nearer to the least degree of satisfaction upon the subject. Contrivance is still unaccounted for. We still want a contriver. A designing mind is neither supplied by this supposition nor dispensed with. If the difficulty were diminished the farther we went back, by going back indefinitely we might exhaust it. And this is the only case to which this sort of reasoning applies. Where there is a tendency, or, as we increase the number of terms, a continual approach toward a limit, *there*, by supposing the number of terms to be what is called infinite, we may conceive the limit to be attained; but where there is no such tendency or approach, nothing is effected by lengthening the series. There is no difference as to the point in question, whatever there may be as to many points, between one series and another—between a series which is finite and a series which is infinite. A chain composed of an infinite number of links can no more support itself than a chain composed of a finite number of links. And of this we are assured, though we never *can* have tried the experiment; because, by increasing the number of links, from ten, for instance, to a hundred, from a hundred to a thousand, etc., we make not the smallest approach, we observe not the smallest tendency toward self-support. There is no difference in this respect—yet there may be a great difference in several respects—between a chain of a greater or less length, between one chain and another, between one that is finite and one that is infinite. This very much resembles the case before us. The machine which we are inspecting demonstrates, by its construction, contrivance and design. Contrivance must have had a contriver, design a designer, whether the machine immediately proceeded from another machine or not. That circumstance alters not the case. That other machine may, in like manner, have proceeded from a former machine: nor does that alter the case; the contrivance must have had a contriver. That former one from one preceding it: no alteration still; a contriver is still necessary. No tendency is perceived, no approach toward a diminution of this necessity. It is the same with any and every succession of these machines—a succession of ten, of a hundred, of a thousand; with one series, as with another—a series which is finite, as with a series which is infinite. In whatever other respects they may differ, in this they do not. In all equally, contrivance and design are unaccounted for. . . .

V. Our observer would further also reflect that the maker of the watch before him was in truth and reality the maker of every watch produced from it: there being no difference, except that the latter manifests a more exquisite skill, between the making of another watch with his own hands, by the mediation of files, lathes, chisels, etc., and the disposing, fixing, and inserting of these instruments, or of others equivalent to them, in the body of the watch already made, in such a manner as to form a new watch in the course of the movements which he had given to the old one. It is only working by one set of tools instead of another. . . .

The Works of Nature

Every observation which was made in our first chapter concerning the watch may be repeated with strict propriety concerning the eye, concerning animals, concerning plants, concerning, indeed, all the organized parts of the works of nature. As,

I. When we are inquiring simply after the *existence* of an intelligent Creator, imperfection, inaccuracy, liability to disorder, occasional irregularities may subsist in a considerable degree without inducing any doubt into the question; just as a watch may frequently go wrong, seldom perhaps exactly right, may be faulty in some parts, defective in some, without the smallest ground of suspicion from thence arising that it was not a watch, not made, or not made for the purpose ascribed to it. When faults are pointed out, and when a question is started concerning the skill of the artist or the dexterity with which the work is executed, then, indeed, in order to defend these qualities from accusation, we must be able either to expose some intractableness and imperfection in the materials or point out some invincible difficulty in the execution, into which imperfection and difficulty the matter of complaint may be resolved; or, if we cannot do this, we must adduce such specimens of consummate art and contrivance proceeding from the same hand as may convince the inquirer of the existence, in the case before him, of impediments like those which we have mentioned, although, what from the nature of the case is very likely to happen, they be unknown and unperceived by him. This we must do in order to vindicate the artist's skill, or at least the perfection of it; as we must also judge of his intention and of the provisions employed in fulfilling that intention, not from an instance in which they fail but from the great plurality of instances in which they succeed. But, after all, these are different questions from the question of the artist's existence; or, which is the same, whether the thing before us be a work of art or not; and the questions ought always to be kept separate in the mind. So likewise it is in the works of nature. Irregularities and imperfections are of little or no weight in the consideration when that consideration relates simply to the existence of a Creator. When the argument respects his attributes, they are of weight; but are then to be taken in conjunction—the attention is not to rest upon them, but they are to be taken in conjunction with the unexceptional evidences which we possess of skill, power, and benevolence displayed in other instances; which evidences may, in strength, number, and variety, be such and may so overpower apparent blemishes as to induce us, upon the most reasonable ground, to believe that these last ought to be referred to some cause, though we be ignorant of it, other than defect of knowledge or of benevolence in the author.

The Earth May Be Very Young

Harold S. Slusher

Scientific Creationism and the theory of Natural Selection make very different predictions concerning the age of the earth. Since evolution is a gradual process, it requires a great deal of time. So, if Darwin's theory is correct, the earth must be very old. On the other hand, if species were created directly by God, the earth could be quite young. Some Creationists even subscribe to the view that the earth is as young as six thousand years old—just old enough to accommodate recorded human history. Physicists generally date the age of rocks using rates of radioactive decay. According to these radiometric dating methods, the earth is roughly 4.5 billion years old, which allows plenty of time for evolution. Creationists, however, challenge the reliability of these methods.

In this selection Harold S. Slusher explains the principles of radiometric dating. He then argues that radioactive decay does not occur at a constant rate, so it cannot be used as a reliable "clock" for dating the age of the earth.

Harold S. Slusher, *Critique of Radiometric Dating*. San Diego: Creation-Life Publishers, Inc., 1973. Copyright © 1973 by Creation-Life Publishers, Inc. Reproduced by permission of the author.

Slusher is an assistant professor of physics at the University of Texas, El Paso. His Ph.D. in geophysics was earned at Columbia Pacific University.

Geologic clocks work on the assumption that some physical quantity is being produced at a constant rate. The clock can give the elapsed time if we know how much of the physical quantity was present when the clock started (Qo), its rate of production (R), and the present amount of the quantity (Q). Looking at this in a simplified form, all we would need to do to find the geologic time (t) by this clock is to divide the amount of the physical quantity produced (ΔQ) during some time interval (t) by its constant rate (R) or production of, $t = {}^{\Delta Q}/_R = {}^{Q - Qo}/_R. \ldots$

Since [American chemist Bertram Borden] Boltwood's determination of alleged ages for ten minerals in 1907, the major radiometric time clocks for geological dating used until recent times have been the uranium (U)—thorium (Th)—lead (Pb) series. These series are thought to constitute three independent clocks: U^{238} decays through several elements to give Pb^{206} and 8 helium nuclei; U^{235} gives Pb^{207} and 7 helium nuclei; and Th^{232} gives Pb^{208} and 6 helium nuclei.

Variability of Radioactive Decay

In order for these radioactive decay families to give the age of a mineral (the time elapsed since the mineral crystallized) the following must be known:

a. The half-lives of U and Th must be determined. These quantities can be determined in the laboratory. [Geologist] Henry Faul says: "Most of the common decay constants have assigned errors of 2 percent or less (standard deviation), but the uncertainty in the decay constant of rubidium-87 is much greater. The two values now in use differ by 6 percent."

b. The decay constants of the radioactive minerals must be constant with time. Radiometric dating is predicated on the assumption that throughout the earth's history radioactive decay rates of the various elements . . . have remained constant. Is this a warranted assumption? Has every radioactive nuclide proceeded on a rigid course of decay at a constant rate? Very recently this has been challenged by a study involving C^{14}. . . .

At any temperature or pressure, collisions with stray cosmic rays or the emanations of other atoms may cause changes other than those of normal disintegration. It seems very possible that what is called "spontaneous disintegration" of radioactive elements is related in some way to the action of cosmic rays and, if so, the rate of disintegration may vary from century to century according to the intensity of the rays. The evidence for a strongly increasing change in the cosmic ray influx is most favorable in the light of [Creationist] Dr. T.G. Barnes' investigation of the decay of the earth's magnetic field.

Most geochronologists maintain that pleochroic haloes give evidence that decay constants have not changed. Crystals of biotite, for example, and other minerals in igneous or metamorphic rocks commonly enclose minute specks of minerals containing uranium or thorium. The α-particles emitted at high velocity by the disintegrating nuclides interact, because of their charge, with electrons of surrounding atoms which slow them down until they finally come to rest in the host mineral at a distance from their source that depends on their initial kinetic energy and the density and composition of the host. Where they finally stop to produce lattice distortions and defects there generally occurs discoloring or darkening. Each of the 8 α-particles emitted during the disintegration of U^{238} to Pb^{206} produces a dark ring in biotite. Each ring has its own characteristic radius in a given mineral (in this case biotite). This radius measures the kinetic energy, hence the probability of emission of the corresponding α-particle and also the half-life of the parent nuclide according to the Geiger-Nuttall law [named after physicists Hans Geiger and J.M. Nuttall]. The Geiger-Nuttall law is an empirical relation between the half-life of the α-emitter and the range in air of the emitted α-particles. If the radii of these haloes from the same nuclide vary, this would imply that the decay rates have varied and would invalidate these series as being actual clocks. Are the radii in the rocks constant in size or are there variable sizes?

Most of the early studies of pleochroic haloes were made by [Irish geologist John] Joly and [Canadian physicist G.H.] Henderson. Joly concluded that the decay rates have varied on the basis of his finding a variation of the radii for rocks of the alleged geological ages. This rather damaging result was explained away handily by saying that "enough evidence of correct radii for different geologic periods and sufficient variation in the same period have been obtained that one is forced to look for a different explanation of such variations as were observed by Joly."

Dr. Roy M. Allen made measurements in an excellent collection of samples with haloes. He found that "the extent of the haloes around the inclusions varies over a wide range, even with the same nuclear material in the same matrix, but all sizes fall into definite groups. My measurements are, in microns, 5, 7, 10, 17, 20, 23, 27, and 33."

Most recent studies have been made by [geophysicist] Robert V. Gentry. Gentry also finds a variation in the haloes leading him to conclude that the decay constants have not been constant in time.

Incidentally, Gentry points out a very telling argument for an instantaneous fiat creation of the earth. He notes from his studies of haloes: "It thus appears that short half-life nuclides of either polonium, bismuth, or lead were incorporated into halo nuclei at the time of mica crystallization and significantly enough existed without the parent nuclides of the uranium series. For the Po^{218} (half-life of 3 minutes) only a matter of minutes could elapse between the formation of the Po^{218} and subsequent crystallization of the mica; otherwise the Po^{218} would have decayed, and no ring would be visible. The occurrence of these halo types is quite widespread, one or more types having been observed in the micas from Canada (Pre-Cambrian), Sweden, and Japan." The argument seems hard to refute.

So, then, careful scientists have measured variations in halo radii and their measurements indicate a variation in decay rates. The radio-active series then would have no value as time clocks.

c. The final and initial concentrations of U and Th in the sample must be known. . . . The final concentrations of U and Th can be determined quite accurately but the determination of U_o and Th_o is based upon assumptions which do not appear to be valid. If theoretical models of nucleosynthesis (formation of elements) and crustal formation are devised and the quantities of Pb^{206}, Pb^{207}, Pb^{208}, and He^4 produced by decay in the sample are known, a set of figures may be calculated regarding the initial concentrations of U and Th in the sample. They are actually only guesses. . . .

Other Sources of Error in Dating Methods

However, aside from the difficulty of finding initial quantities by using models that are pure guesses about the early crust of the earth, there are also basic difficulties in finding the amounts of Pb^{206}, Pb^{207}, Pb^{208}, and He^4 produced by radioactive decay for the following reasons.

1. It is possible and very likely that not all of the Pb^{206},

Pb^{207}, Pb^{208}, and He^4, the decay products of U and Th, found in the samples were produced by radioactive decay. A part of each of the lead isotopes may have been original lead. The helium could have been present when the rocks were formed and not produced at all by radioactive disintegration.

2. There are physical and chemical changes taking place in the crust of the earth that have nothing to do with radioactive decay. For example, helium escapes at a very rapid rate from the rocks into the atmosphere of the earth. It has been estimated that 10,000 to 100,000 tons of helium are exuded into the atmosphere from the rocks each year. U is being carried into the oceans from the rocks at a rate variously estimated from 10,000 to 5,000,000 tons per year. Also, meteors, meteorites, and micrometeorites are bringing U and Th into the atmosphere and onto the surface of the earth. Further, U and Th are brought to the surface by volcanic action. These changes will affect the correctness of the measured amounts of U and Th, thus producing error in the equations for the time calculations. If the amount of U or Th is smaller because of these physical chemical effects, this will give appearance of greater age by radioactive decay.

Obviously, there are major uncertainties and likely errors which can lead to vastly incorrect ages.

d. Appreciable differentiation no doubt has occurred. Many of the uranium salts are water soluble, especially in water containing dissolved oxygen under pressure. These salts migrate with water very readily, both on the surface and underground, until they enter a reducing environment. [Geophysicist F.W.] Hurley has pointed out that the radioactive components of granites reside almost entirely on the grain surface and may readily be leached from the granite. It would appear that a tremendous amount of differentiation has taken place during the lifetimes of the rocks. . . .

It appears that geochronology is an example of a mixture of assumptions, guesses, and imposed imagined universal principles. It would seem that the case of modern geochronology is established in the manner of Mr. Enlightenment's statement in [Christian writer] C.S. Lewis' *Pilgrim's Regress*: "Hypothesis, my dear young friend, establishes itself by a cumulative process: or, to use popular language, if you make the same guess often enough it ceases to be a guess and becomes a Scientific Fact. . . . But when you have had a scientific training you will find that you can be quite certain about all sorts of things which now seem to you only probable."

The Story of Noah's Flood Can Explain the Facts of Natural History

John C. Whitcomb and Henry M. Morris

Not all creationists base their views on a literal interpretation of the Bible, but many do. Such creationists believe that Noah's flood covered the whole earth, not just a local area. They believe the global flood explains many important facts of geology and natural history. The best statement of the creationist flood theory is developed by John C. Whitcomb and Henry M. Morris in their book *The Genesis Flood*.

John C. Whitcomb is a retired professor of theology at Grace Theological Seminary in Indiana. His other books include *The World That Perished* and *The Origin of the Solar System*. Henry M. Morris holds a Ph.D. in Hydraulic Engineering and was head of the Department of Civil Engineering at Virginia Polytechnic Institute and Virginia Tech. He is the founder of the Institute for Creation Research in El Cajon, California, and author of *Scientific Creationism,* a textbook on creationism for students.

In this selection Whitcomb and Morris propose that the Biblical flood story can be taken literally as a record of actual events. They also argue that the distribution of species now observed on earth is consistent with a migration that began on Mt. Ararat.

[The] problem is the capacity of the Ark for carrying two of every kind of land animal and seven of every "clean beast" (Gen. 7:2–3). Realizing full well that the Ark was a gigantic structure, advocates of a local Flood have had to resort to various methods of "multiplying the species" in order to make it impossible for any ark, however large, to carry two of each kind. One method has been to take the phrase "seven and seven" (Gen. 7:2–3) to mean fourteen, instead of "by sevens," and to classify all the birds of the heavens as "clean." Jan Lever, Professor of Zoology at the Free University of Amsterdam, has done this and comes to the conclusion that "of the clean animals and of the birds there were seven pairs, of the unclean one pair. There are known at present about 15,000 species of birds. This means that there were 210,000 birds in the ark."

The Capacity of the Ark

But even assuming that there *were* 15,000 different species of birds in the days of Noah, Dr. Lever has put 180,000 too many birds into the Ark! The Hebrew phrase "seven and seven" no more means fourteen than does the parallel phrase "two and two" (Gen. 7:9,15) mean four! Furthermore, the context demands that the birds were to be classified into "clean" and "unclean" just like the other animals. [Old Testament scholar H.C.] Leupold explains:

> The Hebrew expression "take seven seven" means "seven each." Hebrew parallels support this explanation. In any case, it would be a most clumsy method of trying to say "fourteen." Three pairs and one supernumerary make the "seven." As has often been suggested, the supernumerary beast was the one Noah could conveniently offer for sacrifice after the termination of the Flood. In verse 3 the idea of "the birds of the heavens" must, of course, be supplemented by the adjective "clean," according to the principle laid down in verse 2. The birds are separately mentioned so that Noah might not be left to his own devices in fixing the limits of what verse 2 included.

Another common method of "multiplying the species" has been to identify the "species" of modern taxonomy with the "kinds" of Genesis. John Pye Smith [19th-century theologian] seemed to find much delight in pointing out that the Ark was too small for such a cargo, for "the innumerable millions upon millions of animalcules must be provided for; for they have all their appropriate and diversified places and circumstances of existence."

But a hundred years of further study in the science of zoology has brought to light some interesting facts concerning the amazing potentialities for diversification which the Creator has placed within the Genesis kinds. These "kinds" have never evolved or merged into each other by crossing over the divinely-established lines of demarcation; but they have been diversified into so many varieties and subvarieties (like the races and families of humanity) that even the greatest taxonomists have been staggered at the task of enumerating and classifying them. . . .

It is unwarranted to insist that all the present species, not to mention all the varieties and sub-varieties of animals in the world today, were represented in the Ark. Nevertheless, as a gigantic barge, with a volume of 1,396,000 cubic feet (assuming one cubit = 17.5 inches), the Ark had a carrying capacity equal to that of 522 standard stock cars as used by modern railroads or of eight freight trains with sixty-five such cars in each!

Ernst Mayr, probably the leading American systematic taxonomist, lists the following numbers for animal species according to the best estimates of modern taxonomy:

Mammals	3,500
Birds	8,600
Reptiles & Amphibians	5,500
Fishes	18,000
Tunicates, etc.	1,700
Echinoderms	4,700
Arthropods	815,000
Mollusks	88,000
Worms, etc.	25,000
Coelenterates, etc.	10,000
Sponges	5,000
Protozoans	15,000
TOTAL ANIMALS	1,000,000

In the light of this recent estimate, one wonders about "the innumerable millions upon millions of animalcules" which Pye Smith insisted the Ark had to carry, especially when we consider that of this total there was no need for Noah to make any provision for *fishes* (18,000 "species"), *tunicates* (marine chordates like sea squirts—1,700), *echinoderms* (marine creatures like starfishes and sea urchins—4,700), *mollusks* (mussels, clams, oysters, etc.—88,000), *coelenterates* (corals, sea anemones, jelly fishes, hydroids—10,000), *sponges* (5,000), or *protozoans* (microscopic, single-celled creatures, mostly marine—15,000). This eliminates 142,000 "species" of marine creatures. In addition, some *mammals* are aquatic (whales, seals, porpoises, etc.); the *amphibians* need not all have been included; a large number of the *arthropods* (815,000 "species"), such as lobsters, shrimps, crabs, water fleas, and barnacles, are marine creatures, and the insect "species" among arthropoda are usually very small; and many of the 25,000 "species" of *worms*, as well as many of the insects, could have survived outside of the Ark. When we consider further that Noah was not required to take the largest or even adult specimens of each "kind" and that comparatively few were classified as "clean" birds and beasts, the problem vanishes. Jan Lever completely misses the mark when he states that "the lowest estimate of the number of animals in the ark then would be fully 2,500,000."

For all practical purposes, one could say that, at the outside, there was need for no more than 35,000 individual vertebrate animals on the Ark. The total number of so-called species of mammals, birds, reptiles and amphibians listed by Mayr is 17,600, but undoubtedly the number of original "kinds" was less than this. Assuming the average size of these animals to be about that of a sheep (there are only a very few really large animals, of course, and even these could have been represented on the Ark by young ones), the following will give an idea of the accommodations available:

> The number of animals per car varies greatly, depending on the size and age of the animals. . . . Reports of stock cars and railroads show that the average number of meat animals to the carload is for cattle about 25, hogs in single deck cars about 75, and sheep about 120 per deck.

This means that at least 240 animals of the size of sheep could be accommodated in a standard two-decked stock car. Two trains hauling 73 such cars each would thus be ample to carry the 35,000 animals. We have already seen that the Ark had a carrying capacity equivalent to that of 522 stock cars of this size! We therefore find that a few simple calculations dispose of this trivial objection once and for all.

With respect to the survival of plants through the Flood, we have this comment from Walter E. Lammerts, consultant in the Horticultural Research Division of Germain's, Inc.:

> I am convinced that many thousands of plants survived ei-
> ther as floating vegetation rafts or by chance burial near
> enough to the surface of the ground for asexual sprouting of
> new shoots. I am, of course, aware that objections could be
> raised on the idea that long exposure to salt water would be
> so harmful to any vegetation as to either kill it or so reduce
> its vitality as to make root and new shoot formation impos-
> sible. However, I see no reason at all to postulate that the
> salt content of the ocean at the time of the flood was as high
> as it is now. In fact, on the basis of the canopy theory, we
> would most certainly expect that the salt content of the
> ocean before the flood would be diluted, perhaps by one-
> half. Naturally, during the first few hundred years after the
> flood the salt content of the ocean would again be rather
> rapidly raised because of the much above normal drainage
> of the land surface.

[Creationist Frank Lewis] Marsh further suggests that:

> There was doubtless a considerable number of plants which
> were carried through the Flood in the form of seeds which
> composed a portion of the large store of food cached in the
> ark. But most of the vegetation sprang up here and there
> wherever the propagules were able to survive the Flood.

Caring for the Animals in the Ark

Granting, then, that the Ark was large enough to carry two
of every kind of land animal, how could Noah and his family have cared for them during the year of the Flood? Ramm
fears that "the task of carrying away the manure, and bringing food would completely overtax the few people in the
ark," and quotes F. H. Woods in the *Hastings Encyclopedia of
Religion and Ethics* to the effect that not even the most skilled
modern zoologists could have coped with such a task. [An-
thropologist and Christian writer] Arthur Custance multi-
plies the difficulties even more:

> Many commentators have calculated the size of the Ark and
> the total number of species in the world, and spoken freely

of its capacity to carry them. What they do not always remember is that such animals need attention and food, the carnivorous ones, if they existed as such, requiring meat which would have to be stored up for one whole year. In any case, a sufficient supply of water for drinking would probably have to be taken on board since the mingling of the waters in a worldwide Flood would presumably render it unfit to drink . . . It is rather difficult to visualize a Flood of worldwide proportions but with so little turbulence that four men (perhaps helped by their womenfolk) were able to care for such a flock. It would take very little unsteadiness to make the larger animals almost unmanageable. It becomes even more difficult to conceive how proper provision could have been made for many animals which spend much of their time in the water, such as crocodiles, seals, and so forth.

Since the Bible does not give us details on these points, we are of course unable to speak dogmatically as to the methods which were used in caring for the animals. We suggest the reasonable possibility, however, that the mysterious and remarkable factor of animal physiology known as *hibernation* may have been involved. There are various types of dormancy in animals, with many different types of physiologic and metabolic responses, but it is still an important and widespread mechanism in the animal kingdom for surviving periods of climatic adversity.

> Hibernation and estivation occur in every group of vertebrates save birds, and its pre-disposing causes, immediate and remote, are by no means uniform.

Hibernation is usually associated with "winter sleep," estivation with escape from summer heat and drought. Other factors also apparently are often involved, such as food shortage, carbon dioxide in the environment, and accumulation of fat. Practically all reptiles and amphibians have the capacity of hibernation. Mammals, being warm-blooded, do not have as great a need for it, and so at present, relatively few practice it. Nevertheless, it is probable that the latent ability to do so is present in practically all mammals.

> The zoological dispersion of hibernation among mammals is not especially illuminating, since closely allied forms may differ radically in this respect. Hibernation is reported for the orders Monotremata, Marsupiala, Insectivora, Chiroptera, Rodentia, and Carnivora.

Similarly, many of the invertebrates hibernate in some fashion for long periods. Although it is sometimes said that birds do not hibernate, it is now known that at least one bird, the poor-will, does so, and the humming-bird also exhibits nightly many of the characteristics of hibernation, so that fundamentally it can be said that birds also possess the latent capacity of hibernation. Apparently, the reason more of them do not practice it is that their power of flight makes long migrations a more effective means of coping with adverse weather and other conditions. . . .

We suggest that these remarkable abilities of animals were unusually intensified during the Deluge period. In fact, it may well have been at this time that these powers were first imparted to the animals by God. It seems rather likely that climatic conditions before the Flood were so equable that these particular abilities were not needed then. Perhaps it is significant that, after the Flood, God's pronouncement that "cold and heat, and summer and winter" (Gen. 8:22) would henceforth come in regular cycles is immediately followed by statements concerning the animals that seem to imply changes in animal natures and relationships to mankind (Gen. 9:2–5).

Even as God instructed Noah, by specific revelation, concerning the coming Flood and his means of escape from it, so He instructed certain of the animals, through impartation of a migratory directional instinct which would afterward be inherited in greater or less degree by their descendants, to flee from their native habitats to the place of safety.

Then, having entered the Ark, they also received from God the power to become more or less dormant, in various ways, in order to be able to survive for the year in which they were to be confined within the Ark while the great storms and convulsions raged outside. . . .

Postdiluvian Animal Distribution

A problem which is closely related to the one just discussed, and yet one which demands separate attention, is that of animal distribution throughout the earth since the time of the Flood. If the Flood was geographically universal, then all the air-breathers of the animal kingdom which were not in the Ark perished; and present-day animal distribution must be explained on the basis of migrations from the mountains of Ararat.

In order to have this problem set clearly before us, we shall mention here just two groups of animals, the *edentates* and the *marsupials*. The edentates are slow-moving, nearly toothless animals, some of which are to be found in the jungles of South America (tree sloths, armadillos, and anteaters). How could they have travelled so far from the Near East? The marsupials, or pouched-mammals, are found only in Australia and the Western Hemisphere. How is this peculiarity of animal distribution to be explained?

There are three generally accepted views as to how such animal distribution came about. First, we have the evangelical advocates of a local Flood, who claim that most of these animals were probably created in the ecological niches where they are now found. Secondly, we have the advocates of a universal Flood, who believe that these animals must have reached their present locations by waves of migration during the centuries that followed the Flood. And thirdly, we have the evolutionary school of modern science, which explains such distribution on the basis of gradual processes of migration over millions of years, together with the evolution of totally new kinds of animals in geographically isolated areas.

An unusual feature of this division of opinion is that, in certain respects, most advocates of a universal Flood join the evolutionists in contending for the migration of animals from distant areas, as opposed to the theory of a special creation of animals in their *present* (postdiluvian) ecological zones. Both the evolutionist and the universal Flood advocate claim that inter-continental land bridges have aided animals in their migratory movements across the face of the earth. There are, however, two important differences between these two schools of thought: (1) the evolutionist allows for millions of years, rather than merely thousands, for the present distribution of animals, and (2) the evolutionist allows for the development of different *kinds* of animals instead of holding to the fixity of kinds throughout the entire period of animal distribution. . . .

The marsupials of Australia consist of very distinct types which find their parallels among the placental animals. For example, there are marsupial *moles*, marsupial *anteaters*, marsupial *mice*, marsupial *squirrels* (flying phalangers), marsupial *sloths* (koalas), marsupial *gophers* (wombats), marsupial *cats* (dasyures), marsupial *wolves* (thylacines), marsupial *monkeys*, marsupial *badgers* (Tasmanian devils), strange *lizard-like* marsupials called bandicoots, and the *rabbit-like* kangaroos and wallabies. In addition, Australia boasts the only monotremes (egg-laying mammals) in the world: the duck-billed platypus and the spiny anteater.

On the assumption that the animals of the present world trace their ancestry back to those within the Ark, how can we explain the facts that these marsupials and monotremes are found nowhere in the world except in Australia and that the placentals never succeeded in reaching that subcontinent? John W. Klotz, Professor of Natural History at Concordia Senior College, suggests:

> It may be that these forms have become extinct in Asia and along the Malay Peninsula. Possibly they were able to live in some of these areas for only a very short time and travelled almost immediately to those places included in their present range. The evolutionary scheme itself requires that animals have become extinct in many areas in which they once lived.

A. Franklin Shull, Professor of Zoology at the University of Michigan, has touched upon a very plausible solution to this problem:

> The marsupials spread over the world, in all directions. They could not go far to the north before striking impossible climate, but the path south was open all the way to the tips of Africa and South America and through Australia . . . The placental mammals proved to be superior to the marsupials in the struggle for existence and drove the marsupials out . . . that is, forced them southward. Australia was then connected by land with Asia, so that it could receive the fugitives . . . Behind them the true mammals were coming; but before the latter reached Australia, that continent was separated from Asia, and the primitive types to the south were protected from further competition.

Since fossil marsupials have been found in Europe, as well as in Australia and the Western Hemisphere, it seems evident that they have migrated widely in the past. [Biologist Russel L.] Mixter quotes [marine geologist] A.M. Davies as saying that "they probably reached Europe from North America, but whether they originated in the Northern or Southern Hemisphere, whether in Australia or South America is a matter for guesswork in view of the small amount of evidence."

But what right does one have to map out trans-Asiatic migrations for some marsupials (from North America to Europe) in spite of a lack of fossil evidence for such animals in Asia and then insist that other marsupials could not have migrated from Asia to Australia because of a lack of fossil evidence for marsupials in Asia? Since we have such "a small amount of evidence" to explain marsupial migrations anyway, who can say that marsupials could not have migrated into Australia? The Old Testament informs us that Palestine was infested with lions for centuries (Judges 14:5, I Sam. 17:34, II Sam. 23:20, I Kings 13:24, 20:36, and especially II Kings 17:25), but where is the fossil evidence for their having been in Palestine? It is a well-known fact that animals leave fossil remains only under rare and special conditions. Therefore, the lack of fossil evidence for marsupials in southern Asia cannot be used as proof that they have never been in that region of the world.

Dr. Mixter certainly has no warrant for his assertion that if kangaroos were in the Ark, "they hurried from Australia to meet Noah, and as rapidly returned to their native land." The universal Flood concept by no means involves such absurdities. In the first place, no one can prove that the Ark was built in the same region of the world as that in which it landed. As a matter of fact, if the Flood was universal, antediluvian geography may well have been different from that of the present earth. In the second place, no one can prove that kangaroos and the other Australian marsupials were confined to Australia *before* the Flood. And if not, then none of the chosen pairs of marsupials would have had to "hurry" to get to the Ark during the 120 years that it was under construction. In the third place, it is not necessary to suppose that the very same pair of kangaroos that were in the Ark had to travel all the way to Australia after the Ark landed in the mountains of Ararat. . . .

The more we study the fascinating story of animal distribution around the earth, the more convinced we have become that this vast river of variegated life forms, moving ever outward from the Asiatic mainland, across the continents and seas, has not been a chance and haphazard phenomenon. Instead, we see the hand of God guiding and directing these creatures in ways that man, with all his ingenuity, has never been able to fathom, in order that the great commission to the postdiluvian animal kingdom might be carried out, and "that they may breed abundantly in the earth, and be fruitful, and multiply upon the earth" (Gen. 8:17).

Evolution Violates the Laws of Thermodynamics

Duane T. Gish

Much of the debate between Darwinists and creationists hinges on whether either can claim to be "scientific." Generally, a scientific theory should (1) appeal to forces that can be observed and subjected to experimental studies, (2) make "predictions," and (3) not involve violations of the laws of nature. Creationists admit that their own theory does not always meet these criteria; but, then, neither does the theory of natural selection.

Duane T. Gish holds a Ph.D. in biochemistry from the University of California, Berkeley. He is the author of numerous peer-reviewed articles on biochemistry and has served as a fellow of the National Institute of Health. He is associate director of the Institute for Creation Research in El Cajon, California.

In this selection Gish makes the case that the theory of

Duane T. Gish, "Creationist Science and Education," *Philosophy & Contemporary Issues*, edited by John R. Burr and Milton Goldinger. New York: Prentice-Hall, 1984. Copyright © 1984 by Prentice-Hall. Reproduced by permission of Prentice-Hall/A Division of Simon and Schuster, Upper Saddle River, NJ.

evolution is just as "unscientific" as creationism. He argues that the process of evolution has never been observed. Its central principle, "survival of the fittest," is merely a tautology (an instance of circular reasoning) that makes no testable predictions. Finally, the theory is actually inconsistent with established scientific laws, notably the second law of thermodynamics.

It is commonly believed that the theory of evolution is the only scientific explanation of origins and that the theory of special creation is based solely on religious beliefs. It is further widely accepted that the theory of evolution is supported by such a vast body of scientific evidence, while encountering so few contradictions, that evolution should be accepted as an established fact. As a consequence, it is maintained by many educators that the theory of evolution should be included in science textbooks as the sole explanation for origins but that the theory of special creation, if taught at all, must be restricted to social science courses.

As a matter of fact, neither evolution nor creation qualifies as a scientific theory. Furthermore, it has become increasingly apparent that there are a number of irresolvable contradictions between evolution theory and the facts of science, and that the mechanism postulated for the evolutionary process could account for no more than trivial changes.

It would be well at this point to define what we mean by creation and evolution. By *Creation* we are referring to the theory that the universe and all life forms came into existence by the direct creative acts of a Creator external to and independent of the natural universe. It is postulated that the basic plant and animal kinds were separately created, and that any variation or speciation that has occurred since creation has been limited within the circumscribed boundaries of these created kinds. It is further postulated that the earth has suffered at least one great world-wide catastrophic event or flood which would account for the mass death, destruction, and extinction found on such a monumental scale in geological deposits.

By *Evolution* we are referring to the General Theory of Evolution. This is the theory that all living things have arisen by naturalistic, mechanistic processes from a single primeval cell, which in turn had arisen by similar processes from a dead, inanimate world. This evolutionary process is postulated to have occurred over a period of many hundreds of millions of years. It is further postulated that all major geological formations can be explained by present processes acting essentially at present rates without resort to any world-wide catastrophe(s).

Creation has not been observed by human witnesses. Since creation would have involved unique, unrepeatable historical events, creation is not subject to the experimental method. Furthermore, creation as a theory is non-falsifiable. That is, it is impossible to conceive an experiment that could disprove the possibility of creation. Creation thus does not fulfill the criteria of a scientific theory. That does not say anything about its ultimate validity, of course. Furthermore, creation theory can be used to correlate and explain data, particularly that available from the fossil record, and is thus subject to test in the same manner that other alleged historical events are subject to test—by comparison with historical evidence.

Evolution theory also fails to meet the criteria of a scientific theory. Evolution has never been witnessed by human observers; evolution is not subject to the experimental method; and as formulated by present-day evolutionists, it has become non-falsifiable.

Evolution Has Never Been Observed

It is obvious that no one has ever witnessed the type of evolutionary changes postulated by the general theory of evolution. No one, for example, witnessed the origin of the universe or the origin of life. No one has ever seen a fish evolve into an amphibian, nor has anyone observed an ape evolve into a man. No one, as a matter of fact, has ever witnessed a significant evolutionary change of any kind. . .

The world-famous evolutionist, Theodosis Dobzhansky, while endeavoring to proclaim his faith in evolution, admitted that no real evolutionary change has ever been observed by man when he said, ". . . the occurrence of the evolution of life in the history of the earth is established about as well as events *not witnessed by human observers can be.*" It can be said with certainty, then, that evolution in the present world has never been observed. It remains as far outside the pale of human observation as the origin of the universe or the origin of life. Evolution has been *postulated* but *never observed.*

Since evolution cannot be observed, it is not amenable to the methods of experimental science. This has been acknowledged by Dobzhansky when he stated, "These evolutionary happenings are unique, unrepeatable, and irreversible. It is as impossible to turn a land vertibrate into a fish as it is to effect the reverse transformation. The applicability of the experimental method to the study of such unique historical processes is severely restricted before all else by the time intervals involved, which far exceed the lifetime of any human experimenter. And yet it is just such *impossibility* that is demanded by antievolutionists when they ask for 'proofs' of evolution which they would magnanimously accept as satisfactory."

Please note that Dobzhansky has said that the applicability of the experimental method to the study of evolution is an impossibility! It is obvious, then, that evolution fails to qualify as a scientific theory, for it is certain that a theory that cannot be subjected to experimental test is not a scientific theory. . . .

Evolution Is a Tautology

The core of modern evolution theory, known as the neo-Darwinian theory of evolution, or the modern synthetic theory, is the hypothesis that the evolutionary process has occurred through natural selection of random mutational changes in the genetic material, selection being in accordance with alterations in the environment. Natural selection, itself, is not a chance process, but the material it must act on, mutant genes, is produced by random, chance processes.

It is an astounding fact that while at the time Darwin popularized it, the concept of natural selection seemed to explain so much, today there is a growing realization that the presently accepted concept of natural selection really explains nothing. It is a mere tautology, that is, it involves circular reasoning.

In modern theory, natural selection is defined in terms of differential reproduction. In fact, according to [zoologist Richard] Lewontin, differential reproduction *is* natural selection. When it is asked, what survives, the answer is, the fittest. But when it is asked, what are the fittest, the answer is, those that survive! Natural selection thus collapses into a tautology, devoid of explanatory value. It is not possible to explain *why* some varieties live to reproduce more offspring—it is only known that they do.

In discussing Richard Levins' concept of fitness set analysis, [biologist William] Hamilton stated, "This criticism amounts to restating what I think is the admission of most evolutionists, that we do not yet know what natural selection maximizes." Now if evolutionists do not know what natural selection maximizes, they do not know what natural selection selects.

In a review of the thinking in French scientific circles, it was stated, "Even if they do not publicly take a definite stand, almost all French specialists hold today strong mental reservations as to the validity of natural selection." Creationists maintain that indeed natural selection could not result in increased complexity or convert a plant or animal into another basic kind. It can only act to eliminate the unfit.

[Creationist Norman] Macbeth has recently published an especially incisive criticism of evolution theory and of the concept of natural selection as used by evolutionists. He points out that although evolutionists have abandoned classical Darwinism, the modern synthetic theory they have proposed as a substitute is equally inadequate to explain progressive change as a result of natural selection, and, as a matter of fact, they cannot even define natural selection in non-tautological terms. Inadequacies of the present theory and failure of the fossil record to substantiate predictions based on the theory leave macro-evolution, and even micro-evolution, intractable mysteries according to Macbeth. Macbeth suggests that no theory at all may be preferable to the present theory of evolution.

Using Macbeth's work as the starting point for his own investigation of modern evolution theory, [creationist Tom] Bethell, a graduate of Oxford with a major in philosophy, has expressed his complete dissatisfaction with the present formulations of evolution theory and natural selection from the viewpoint of the philosophy of science. Both Macbeth and Bethell present excellent reviews of the thinking of leading evolutionists concerning the relationship of natural selection to evolution theory. While both are highly critical, neither profess to be creationists.

According to modern evolutionary theory, ultimately all

of the evolution is due to mutations. Mutations are random changes in the genes or chromosomes which are highly ordered structures. Any process that occurs by random chance events is subject to the laws of probability.

It is possible to estimate mutation rates. It is also possible to estimate how many favorable mutations would be required to bring about certain evolutionary changes. Assuming that these mutations produced in a random, chance manner, as is true in the Neo-Darwinian interpretation of evolution, it is possible to calculate how long such an evolutionary process would have required to convert an amoeba into a man. When this is done, according to a group of mathematicians, all of whom are evolutionists, the answer turns out to be billions of times longer than the assumed five billion years of earth history!

One of these mathematicians, Murray Eden, stated, "It is our contention that if 'random' is given a serious and crucial interpretation from a probabilistic point of view, the randomness postulate is highly implausible and that an *adequate scientific theory of evolution must await the discovery and elucidation of new natural laws—physical, physico-chemical, and biological."* What Eden and these mathematicians are saying is that the modern neo-Darwinian theory of evolution is totally inadequate to explain more than trivial change and thus we simply have no basis at present for attempting to explain how evolution may have occurred. As a matter of fact, based on the assumption that the evolutionary process was dependent upon random chance processes, we can simply state that evolution would have been impossible.

Evolution Violates the Second Law of Thermodynamics

Furthermore, evolution theory contradicts one of the most firmly established laws known to science, the Second Law of

Thermodynamics. The obvious contradiction between evolution and the Second Law of Thermodynamics becomes evident when we compare the definition of this Law and its consequences by several scientists (all of whom, as far as we know, accept evolutionary philosophy) with the definition of evolution by Sir Julian Huxley, biologist and one of the best-known spokesmen for evolution theory.

> There is a general natural tendency of all observed systems to go from order to disorder, reflecting dissipation of energy available for future transformations—the law of increasing entropy.

> All real processes go with an increase of entropy. The entropy also measures the randomness, or lack of orderliness of the system: the greater the randomness, the greater the entropy.

> Another way of stating the second law then is: 'The universe is constantly getting more disorderly!' Viewed that way, we can see the second law all about us. We have to work hard to straighten a room, but left to itself it becomes a mess again very quickly and very easily. Even if we never enter it, it becomes dusty and musty. How difficult to maintain houses, and machinery, and our own bodies in perfect working order: how easy to let them deteriorate. In fact, all we have to do is nothing, and everything deteriorates, collapses, breaks down, wears out, all by itself—and that is what the second law is all about.

Now compare these definitions or consequences of the Second Law of Thermodynamics to the theory of evolution as defined by Huxley:

> Evolution in the extended sense can be defined as a directional and essentially irreversible process occurring in time, which in its course gives rise to an increase of variety and an increasingly high level of organization in its products. Our present knowledge indeed forces us to the view that the whole of reality is evolution—a single process of self-transformation.

There is a natural tendency, then, for all observed natural

systems to go from order to disorder, towards increasing randomness. This is true throughout the entire known universe, both at the micro and macro levels. This tendency is so invariant that it has never been observed to fail. It is a natural law—the Second Law of Thermodynamics.

On the other hand, according to the general theory of evolution, as defined by Huxley, there is a general tendency of natural systems to go from disorder to order, towards an ever higher and higher level of complexity. This tendency supposedly operates in every corner of the universe, both at the micro and macro levels. As a consequence, it is believed, particles have evolved into people.

It is difficult to understand how a discerning person could fail to see the basic contradiction between these two processes. It seems apparent that both cannot be true, but no modern scientist would dare challenge the validity of the Second Law of Thermodynamics.

The usual, but exceedingly naive, answer given by evolutionists to this dilemma is that the Second Law of Thermodynamics applies only to closed systems. If the system is open to an external source of energy, it is asserted, complexity can be generated and maintained within this system at the expense of the energy supplied to it from the outside.

Thus, our solar system is an open system, and energy is supplied to the earth from the sun. The decrease in entropy, or increase in order, on the earth during the evolutionary process, it is said, has been more than compensated by the increase in entropy, or decrease in order, on the sun. The overall result has been a net decrease in order, so the Second Law of Thermodynamics has not been violated, we are told.

An open system and an adequate external source of energy are necessary *but not sufficient* conditions, however, for order to be generated and maintained, since raw, undirected, uncontrolled energy is destructive, not constructive. For example, without the protective layer of ozone in the upper atmosphere which absorbs most of the ultraviolet light coming from the sun, life on earth would be impossible. Bacterial cells exposed to such radiation die within seconds. This is because ultraviolet light, or irradiation of any kind, breaks chemical bonds and thus randomizes and destroys the highly complex structures found in biologically active macromolecules, such as proteins and DNA. Biological activity of these vitally important molecules is destroyed and death rapidly follows.

That much more than merely an external energy source is required to form complex molecules and systems from simpler ones is evident from the following statement by [textbook authors George Gaylord] Simpson and [W.S.] Beck ". . . the simple expenditure of energy is not sufficient to develop and maintain order. A bull in a china shop performs work, but he neither creates nor maintains organization. The work needed is *particular* work; it must follow specifications; it requires information on how to proceed."

Thus a green plant, utilizing the highly complex photosynthetic system it possesses, can trap light energy from the sun and convert this light energy into chemical energy. A series of other complex systems within the green plant allows the utilization of this energy to build up complex molecules and systems from simple starting material. Of equal importance is the fact that the green plant possesses a system for directing, maintaining, and replicating these complex energy conversion mechanisms—an incredibly complex genetic system. Without the genetic system, no specifications on how to proceed would exist, chaos would result, and life would be impossible.

For complexity to be generated within a system, then, four conditions must be met:

1. The system must be an open system.

2. An adequate external energy source must be available.

3. The system must possess energy conversion mechanisms.

4. A control mechanism must exist within the system for directing, maintaining, and replicating these energy conversion mechanisms.

The seemingly irresolvable dilemma, from an evolutionary point of view, is, how such complex energy conversion mechanisms and genetic systems arose in the *absence* of such systems, when there is a general natural tendency to go from order to disorder, a tendency so universal it can be stated as a natural law, the Second Law of Thermodynamics. Simply stated, machines are required to build machines, and something or somebody must operate the machinery.

The creationist thus opposes the wholly unscientific evolutionary hypothesis that the natural universe with all of its incredible complexity, was capable of generating itself, and maintains that there must exist, external to the natural universe, a Creator, or supernatural Agent, who was responsible for introducing, or creating, the high degree of order found within this natural universe. While creationism is extra-scientific, it is not anti-scientific, as is the evolutionary hypothesis which contradicts one of the most well-established laws of science.

Nature Can Be Tested for Intelligent Design

William A. Dembski

Some scientists need to distinguish natural phenomena from phenomena produced by conscious intelligence. Archaeologists, for example, sometimes have to distinguish simple tools, such as hide scrapers and grinding stones, from stone formations caused by the natural fragmentation of rock. Astronomers working for S.E.T.I. (Search for Extra-Terrestrial Intelligence) use sophisticated statistical analysis to look for radio signals that might be produced by intelligent alien life-forms. These same techniques could be used to discover whether intelligent design shapes life on earth.

William A. Dembski received a Ph.D. in philosophy from the University of Illinois at Chicago and a doctorate in mathematics from the University of Chicago. He also has a master's degree from the Princeton Theological Seminary. He is the author of numerous books and articles on philosophy, mathematics, and theology, and he has taught at

William A. Dembski, *No Free Lunch: Why Specified Complexity Cannot Be Purchased Without Intelligence*. Lanham, MD: Rowman & Littlefield Publishers, 2002. Copyright © 2002 by Rowman & Littlefield Publishers, Inc. Reproduced by permission.

Northwestern University, the University of Notre Dame, and the University of Dallas.

In this selection Dembski outlines the rationale for a scientific research program aimed at finding intelligent design in the natural world. He explains what questions such a research program would ask and what impact it would have on related fields of science.

Consider how the radio astronomers in the movie *Contact* detected an extraterrestrial intelligence. This movie, based on a novel by [astronomer] Carl Sagan, was an enjoyable piece of propaganda for the SETI research program—the Search for Extraterrestrial Intelligence. To make the movie interesting, the SETI researchers in *Contact* actually did find an extraterrestrial intelligence (the real-life SETI program has yet to be so lucky).

The Search for Intelligence

How, then, did the SETI researchers in *Contact* convince themselves that they had found an extraterrestrial intelligence? To increase their chances of finding an extraterrestrial intelligence, SETI researchers monitor millions of radio signals from outer space. Many natural objects in space produce radio waves (e.g., pulsars). Looking for signs of design among all these naturally produced radio signals is like looking for a needle in a haystack. To sift through the haystack, SETI researchers run the signals they monitor through computers programmed with pattern-matchers. So long as a signal does not match one of the preset patterns, it will pass through the pattern-matching sieve (even if it has an intelligent source). If, on the other hand, it does match one of these patterns, then, depending on the pattern matched, the

SETI researchers may have cause for celebration.

The SETI researchers in *Contact* did find a signal worthy of celebration, namely the following:

```
110111011111011111110111111111110111111111111011111111
111111111101111111111111111111011111111111111111111111101
111111111111111111111111111011111111111111111111111111111
111110111111111111111111111111111111111111111011111111111
111111111111111111111111111110111111111111111111111111111
111111111111111111101111111111111111111111111111111111111
111111111111101111111111111111111111111111111111111111111
111111111111011111111111111111111111111111111111111111111
111111111111111111011111111111111111111111111111111111111
111111111111111111111111111111110111111111111111111111111
111111111111111111111111111111111111111111111111110111111
111111111111111111111111111111111111111111111111111111111
111111111111011111111111111111111111111111111111111111111
111111111111111111111111111111111111011111111111111111111
111111111111111111111111111111111111111111111111111111111
111111111111011111111111111111111111111111111111111111111
111111111111111111111111111111111111111111111111110111111
111111111111111111111111111111111111111111111111111111111
111111111111111111111111111111111110111111111111111111111
111111111111111111111111111111111111111111111111111111111
111111111111111111111111111
```

The SETI researchers in *Contact* received this signal as a sequence of 1126 beats and pauses, where 1s correspond to beats and 0s to pauses. This sequence represents the prime numbers from 2 to 101, where a given prime number is represented by the corresponding number of beats (i.e., 1s), and the individual prime numbers are separated by pauses (i.e., 0s). Thus the sequence begins with 2 beats, then a pause, 3 beats, then a pause, 5 beats, then a pause, all the way up to 101 beats. The SETI researchers in *Contact* took this signal as decisive confirmation of an extraterrestrial intelligence.

What about this signal indicates design? Whenever we infer design, we must establish three things: *contingency, complexity*, and *specification*. Contingency ensures that the object in question is not the result of an automatic and therefore unintelligent process that had no choice in its production. Complexity ensures that the object is not so simple that it can readily be explained by chance. Finally, specification ensures that the object exhibits the type of pattern characteristic of intelligence. . . .

Outline of a Research Program

Logic does not require that a scientific theory be rejected only after a better alternative is found. It does seem to be a fact about the sociology of science, however, that scientific theories give way not to criticism but to new, improved theories. Informed critiques of Darwinism have consistently appeared ever since Darwin published his *Origin of Species*. . . . Yet all these critiques never succeeded in transforming design into a viable scientific alternative to Darwinism. For intelligent design to succeed as an intellectual project, the crucial next step is therefore to develop a design-theoretic research program as a positive alternative to Darwinism and other naturalistic approaches to the origin and history of life. In broad strokes, such a positive research program is now in place and looks as follows (here I am going to offer a conceptual rather than a historical reconstruction):

1. Much as Darwin began with the commonsense recognition that artificial selection in animal and plant breeding experiments is capable of directing organismal variation (which he then bootstrapped into a general mechanism to account for all organismal variation), so too a design-theoretic research program begins with the commonsense recognition that humans draw design inferences routinely in ordinary life, explaining some things in terms of purely natural causes and other things in terms of intelligence or design (cf. archeologists attributing rock formations in one case to erosion and in another to design—as with the megaliths at Stonehenge).

2. Just as Darwin formalized and extended our common-sense understanding of artificial selection to natural selection, a design-theoretic research program next attempts to formalize and extend our commonsense understanding of design inferences so that they can be rigorously applied in scientific investigation. . . .

3. At the heart of my codification of design inferences is the notion of specified complexity, which is a statistical and complexity-theoretic concept. Provided this concept is well-defined and can effectively be applied in practice, the next question is whether specified complexity is exhibited in actual physical systems where no evolved, reified, or embodied intelligence was involved. In other words, the next step is to apply the codification of design inferences in step 2 to natural systems and see whether it properly leads us to infer design. . . .

Intelligent design is a scientific research program that examines the role of specified complexity in nature. Since many special sciences already employ specified complexity as a criterion for detecting design (e.g., SETI and archeology), there can be no principled objection to teaching intelligent design within a science curriculum, and particularly whenever the origin and history of life comes up in grades K–12. To affirm the legitimacy of intelligent design as a proper subject for study within a science curriculum, however, raises two practical questions: (1) How is intelligent design to be taught? and (2) How will its teaching affect the teaching of other scientific subjects, notably biological evolution? One of the worries about intelligent design is that it will jettison much that is accepted in science, and that an "ID-based curriculum" will look very different from current science curricula. Although intelligent design has radical implications for science, I submit that it does not have nearly as radical implications for science education.

First off, intelligent design is not a form of anti-evolutionism. Intelligent design does not claim that living things came together suddenly in their present form through the efforts of a supernatural creator. Intelligent design is not and never will be a doctrine of creation. A doctrine of creation presupposes not only a designer that in some manner is responsible for organizing the structure of the universe and its various parts but also a creator that is the source of being of the universe. A doctrine of creation thus invariably entails metaphysical and theological claims about a creator and the creation. Intelligent design, on the other hand, merely concerns itself with features of natural objects that reliably signal the action of an intelligence, whatever that intelligence might be. More significantly for the educational curriculum, however, is that intelligent design has no stake in living things coming together suddenly in their present form. To be sure, intelligent design leaves that as a possibility. But intelligent design is also fully compatible with large-scale evolution over the course of natural history, all the way up to what biologists refer to as "common descent" (i.e., the full genealogical interconnectedness of all organisms). If our best science tells us that living things came together gradually over a long evolutionary history and that all living things are related by common descent, then so be it. Intelligent design can live with that result and indeed live with it cheerfully.

But—and this is the crucial place where an ID-based curriculum will differ from how biological evolution is currently taught—intelligent design is not willing to accept common descent as a consequence of the Darwinian mechanism. The Darwinian mechanism claims the power to transform a single organism (known as the last common ancestor) into the full diversity of life that we see both around us and in the fossil record. If intelligent design is correct, then the Darwinian mechanism of natural selection and random variation lacks that power. What's more, in that case the justification for common descent cannot be that it follows as a logical deduction from Darwinism. Darwinism is not identical with evolution understood merely as common descent. Darwinism comprises a historical claim (common descent) and a naturalistic mechanism (natural selection operating on random variations), with the latter being used to justify the former. According to intelligent design, the Darwinian mechanism cannot bear the weight of common descent. Intelligent design therefore throws common descent into question but at the same time leaves open as a very live possibility that common descent is the case, albeit for reasons other than the Darwinian mechanism.

Life Could Not Have Started Randomly

Phillip E. Johnson

Strictly speaking, Darwin's theory does not attempt to explain how life began. It only attempts to explain how complex life-forms might have developed from simple forms. However, Darwinists generally believe that the earliest forms of life might have been so simple that life might have begun by sheer accident. Creationists argue that even the simplest forms of life are so complicated that they could not have started by accident. The origin of even the simplest forms of life would require an act of creation.

In the following passage Phillip E. Johnson reviews current theories for the origin of life and concludes that all the theories so far proposed are wildly speculative and implausible. Johnson has taught law at the University of California at Berkeley for over twenty years. He served as a law clerk for Chief Justice Earl Warren.

Phillip E. Johnson, *Darwin on Trial*. Washington, DC: Henry Regnery Publishing, 1991. Copyright © 1991 by Henry Regnery Publishing. Reproduced by permission.

When the Supreme Court struck down the Louisiana law requiring balanced treatment for creation-science, Justice Antonin Scalia dissented from the decision because he thought that "The people of Louisiana, including those who are Christian fundamentalists, are quite entitled . . . to have whatever scientific evidence there may be against evolution presented in their schools." [Naturalist] Stephen Jay Gould was baffled that a jurist of Scalia's erudition (he had held professorships at several major universities) would entertain the absurd notion that fundamentalists could have scientific evidence against evolution. Gould went looking in Scalia's opinion for an explanation, and found it in various sentences implying that evolution is a theory about the origin of life.

Prebiological Evolution

In an article correcting "Justice Scalia's Misunderstanding," Gould tried to set the matter straight. Evolution, he wrote, "is not the study of life's ultimate origin, as a path toward discerning its deepest meaning." Even the purely scientific aspects of life's first appearance on earth belong to other divisions of science, because "evolution" is merely the study of how life changes once it is already in existence. Because he misunderstood the strictly limited subject matter of evolution, Scalia had tumbled into the misunderstanding that it is possible to have rational objections to the doctrines of evolutionary science.

In fact, Justice Scalia used the general term "evolution" exactly as scientists use it—to include not only *biological* evolution but also *prebiological* or chemical evolution, which seeks to explain how life first evolved from nonliving chemicals. Biological evolution is just one major part of a grand naturalistic project, which seeks to explain the origin of everything from the Big Bang to the present without allowing any role to a Creator. If Darwinists are to keep the Creator out of the picture, they have to provide a naturalistic explanation for the origin of life. . . .

The basic difficulty in explaining how life could have begun is that all living organisms are extremely complex, and Darwinian selection cannot perform the designing even in theory until living organisms already exist and are capable of reproducing their kind. A Darwinist can imagine that a mutant rodent might appear with a web between its toes, and thereby gain some advantage in the struggle for survival, with the result that the new characteristic could spread through the population to await the arrival of further mutations leading eventually to winged flight. The trouble is that the scenario depends upon the rodent having offspring that inherit the mutant characteristic, and chemicals do not produce offspring. The challenge of chemical evolution is to find a way to get some chemical combination to the point where reproduction and selection could get started.

The Primordial Soup

The field achieved its greatest success in the early 1950s when Stanley Miller, then a graduate student in the laboratory of Harold Urey at the University of Chicago, obtained small amounts of two amino acids by sending a spark through a mixture of gases thought to simulate the atmosphere of the early earth. Because amino acids are used in building proteins, they are sometimes called the "building blocks of life." Subsequent experiments based on the Miller-Urey model produced a variety of amino acids and other complex compounds employed in the genetic process, with the result that the more optimistic researchers concluded that the chemicals needed to construct life could have been present in sufficient abundance on the early earth. . . .

Geochemists now report that the atmosphere of the early earth probably was not of the strongly reducing nature required for the Miller-Urey apparatus to give the desired results. Even under ideal and probably unrealistic conditions, the experiments failed to produce some of the necessary chemical components of life. Perhaps the most discouraging criticism has come from chemists, who have spoiled the prebiotic soup by showing that organic compounds produced on the early earth would be subject to chemical reactions making them unsuitable for constructing life. In all probability, the prebiotic soup could never have existed, and without it there is no reason to believe that the production of small amounts of some amino acids by electrical charge in a reducing atmosphere had anything to do with the origin of life.

Although these objections to the significance of the Miller-Urey results are important, for present purposes I prefer to disregard them as a distraction from the main point. Let us grant that, one way or another, all the required chemical components were present on the early earth. That still leaves us at a dead end, because there is no reason to believe that life has a tendency to emerge when the right chemicals are sloshing about in a soup. Although some components of living systems can be duplicated with very advanced techniques, scientists employing the full power of their intelligence cannot manufacture living organisms from amino acids, sugars, and the like. How then was the trick done before scientific intelligence was in existence?

The simplest organism capable of independent life, the prokaryote bacterial cell, is a masterpiece of miniaturized complexity which makes a spaceship seem rather low-tech. Even if one assumes that something much simpler than a bacterial cell might suffice to start Darwinist evolution on its way—a DNA or RNA macromolecule, for example—the possibility that such a complex entity could assemble itself by chance is still fantastically unlikely, even if billions of years had been available.

I won't quote figures because exponential numbers are unreal to people who are not used to them, but a metaphor by Fred Hoyle has become famous because it vividly conveys the magnitude of the problem: that a living organism emerged by chance from a prebiotic soup is about as likely as that "a tornado sweeping through a junkyard might assemble a Boeing 747 from the materials therein." Chance assembly is just a naturalistic way of saying "miracle.". . .

[Evolutionary biologist] Richard Dawkins, who has Darwin's own facility for turning a liability into an asset, has even argued that the improbability of the origin of life scenarios is a point in their favor. He reasons that "An apparently (to ordinary human consciousness) miraculous theory is *exactly* the kind of theory we should be looking for in this particular matter of the origin of life." This is because "evolution has equipped our brains with a subjective consciousness of risk and improbability suitable for creatures with a lifetime of less than one century."

Dawkins is actually *encouraged* by the failure of scientists to duplicate the spontaneous generation of life in their laboratories. After all, scientists can't duplicate biological macroevolution either. If making life were easy enough that scientists could do it, then nature would have caused life to originate spontaneously on earth many times, as well as on planets within radio range. As it appears that this did not happen, failure to duplicate the origin of life in the laboratory is just what Darwinist theory would lead us to expect.

When it becomes necessary to rely on arguments like that one, the experimental work must be going very badly. . . .

Recent Approaches to the Problem

An imaginative idea about what a prebiotic genetic system might have been like has been proposed by A.G. Cairns-Smith, most recently in a charming book titled *Seven Clues to the Origin of Life*. Bizarre as the idea may appear at first, or even upon reflection, Cairns-Smith thinks that clay crystals have qualities that might make possible their combination into a form of pre-organic mineral life. According to Darwinist assumptions, natural selection would then favor the more efficient clay replicators, preparing the way for an eventual "genetic takeover" by organic molecules that had evolved because of their increasing usefulness in the pre-organic process.

The imagination involved in the mineral origin of life thesis is impressive, but for my purpose it is sufficient to say that it is altogether lacking in experimental confirmation. According to the biochemist Klaus Dose, "This thesis is beyond the comprehension of all biochemists or molecular biologists who are daily confronted with the experimental facts of life." That would ordinarily be more than enough reason to discard a theory, but many scientists still take the idea of a mineral origin of life seriously because there is no clearly superior competitor. . . .

Prospects for experimental success are so discouraging that the more enterprising researchers have turned to computer simulations that bypass the experimental roadblocks by employing convenient assumptions. An article in *Science* in 1990 summarized the state of computer research into "spontaneous self-organization," a concept based upon the premise that complex dynamical systems tend to fall into a highly ordered state even in the absence of selection pressures. This premise may seem to contradict the famous Second Law of Thermodynamics, which says that ordered energy inevitably collapses into disorder or maximum "entropy." There is reason to believe, however, that in a local system (the earth) which takes in energy from outside (the sun), the second law permits some kinds of spontaneous self-organization to occur. For example, ordered structures like snowflakes and crystals are common. More to the point, most scientists assume that *life* originated spontaneously and thereafter evolved to its present state of complexity. This could not have happened unless powerful self-organizing tendencies were present in nature.

Starting from assumptions like that, scientists can design computer models that mimic the origin of life and its subsequent evolution. Whether the models have any connection to reality is another question. According to *Science*, "Advocates of spontaneous organization are quick to admit that they aren't basing their advocacy on empirical data and laboratory experiments, but on abstract mathematics and novel computer models." The biochemist G.F. Joyce commented: "They have a long way to go to persuade mainstream biologists of the relevance [of this work]."

Assuming away the difficult points is one way to solve an intractable problem; another is to send the problem off into space. That was the strategy of one of the world's most famous scientists, Francis Crick, co-discoverer of the structure of DNA. Crick is thoroughly aware of the awesome complexity of cellular life and the extreme difficulty of explaining how such life could have evolved in the time available on earth. So he speculated that conditions might have been more favorable on some distant planet.

That move leaves the problem of getting life from the planet of origin to earth. First in a paper with Leslie Orgel, and then in a book of his own, Crick advanced a theory he called "directed pan-spermia." The basic idea is that an advanced extraterrestrial civilization, possibly facing extinction, sent primitive life forms to earth in a spaceship. The spaceship builders couldn't come themselves because of enormous time required for interstellar travel; so they sent bacteria capable of surviving the voyage and the severe conditions that would have greeted them upon arrival on the early earth.

What kind of scientific evidence supports directed pan-spermia? Crick wrote that if the theory is true, we should expect that cellular microorganisms would appear suddenly, without evidence that any simpler forms preceded them. We should also expect to find that the early forms were distantly related but highly distinct, with no evidence of ancestors because these existed only on the original planet. This expectation fits the facts perfectly, because the archae-bacteria and eubacteria are at the same time too different to have evolved from a common ancestor in the time available, and yet also too similar (sharing the same genetic language) not to have a common source somewhere. Those who are tempted to ridicule directed pan-spermia should restrain themselves, because Crick's extraterrestrials are no more invisible than the universe of ancestors that earth-bound Darwinists have to invoke.

Crick would be scornful of any scientist who gave up on scientific research and ascribed the origin of life to a super-natural Creator. But directed pan-spermia amounts to the same thing. The same limitations that made it impossible for the extraterrestrials to journey to earth will make it impossible for scientists ever to inspect their planet. Scientific investigation of the origin of life is as effectively closed off as if God had reserved the subject for Himself.

Darwinism Is Immoral

William Jennings Bryan

The phrase "survival of the fittest," so often associated with Darwinism, seems to suggest that the forces of nature are inclined to reward selfish behavior. From this it seems to follow that, if people accept Darwinism, they will be likely to adopt a personal code of conduct that could only be characterized as un-Christian and immoral. Whether Darwinism is true or false, the teaching of Darwinism could be detrimental to society. This concern is most eloquently expressed by William Jennings Bryan, an early critic of Darwinism. However, the same concern is often expressed by Darwinism's modern critics as well.

William Jennings Bryan (1860–1925) ran for president unsuccessfully three times on the Democratic ticket, in 1896, 1900, and 1908. He considered himself a fundamentalist Christian, but was ahead of his time in advocating liberal governmental policies, including an anti-imperialistic foreign policy and generous social programs to assist the poor. He served as the prosecuting attorney in the 1925 trial

William Jennings Bryan, *The Scopes Trial, Special Edition*. Delran, NJ: Gryphon Editions: The Notable Trials Library, 1990. Copyright © 1990 by The Notable Trials Library, Division of Gryphon Editions. Reproduced by permission.

of schoolteacher John Scopes, accused of breaking the Tennessee law against teaching the theory of evolution. Bryan died less than a week after winning the case.

In this selection, Bryan argues that Darwin himself, and many proponents of Darwin's theory, endorse a morality that is devoid of pity, encourages war and sexual promiscuity, and ultimately threatens to destroy civilization.

The Christians who have allowed themselves to be deceived into believing that evolution is a beneficent, or even a rational process, have been associating with those who either do not understand its implications or dare not avow their knowledge of these implications. Let me give you some authority on this subject. I will begin with Darwin, the high priest of evolution, to whom all evolutionists bow.

Barbarous Sentiments Expressed by Darwin

On pages 149 and 150, in "The Descent of Man," he says:

> With savages, the weak in body or mind are soon eliminated; and those that survive commonly exhibit a vigorous state of health. We civilized men, on the other hand, do our utmost to check the process of elimination; we build asylums for the imbecile, the maimed and the sick; we institute poor laws; and our medical men exert their utmost skill to save the life of everyone to the last moment. There is reason to believe that vaccination has preserved thousands who, from a weak constitution, would formerly have succumbed to smallpox. Thus the weak members of civilized society propagate their kind. No one who has attended to the breeding of domestic animals will doubt that this must be highly injurious to the race of man. It is surprising how soon a want of care, or care wrongly directed, leads to the degeneration of a domestic race; but, excepting in the case of man himself, hardly anyone is so ignorant as to allow his worst animals to breed.

> The aid which we feel impelled to give to the helpless is mainly an incidental result of the instinct of sympathy, which was originally acquired as part of the social instincts, but subsequently rendered in the manner previously indicated more tender and more widely diffused. Nor could we check our sympathy, even at the urging of hard reason, without deterioration in the noblest part of our nature . . . We must, therefore, bear the undoubtedly bad effects of the weak surviving and propagating their kind.

Darwin reveals the barbarous sentiment that runs through evolution and dwarfs the moral nature of those who become obsessed with it. Let us analyze the quotation just given. Darwin speaks with approval of the savage custom of eliminating the weak so that only the strong will survive and complains that "we civilized men do our utmost to check the process of elimination." How inhuman such a doctrine as this! He thinks it injurious to "build asylums for the imbecile, the maimed, and the sick," or to care for the poor. Even the medical men come in for criticism because they "exert their utmost skill to save the life of everyone to the last moment." And then note his hostility to vaccination, because it has "preserved thousands who, from a weak constitution would, but for vaccination, have succumbed to smallpox!" All of the sympathetic activities of civilized society are condemned because they enable "the weak members to propagate their kind." Then he drags mankind down to the level of the brute and compares the freedom given to man unfavorably with the restraint that we put on barnyard beasts.

The second paragraph of the above quotation shows that his kindly heart rebelled against the cruelty of his own doctrine. He says that we "feel impelled to give to the helpless," although he traces it to a sympathy which he thinks is developed by evolution; he even admits that we could not check this sympathy "even at the urging of hard reason, without deterioration of the noblest part of our nature."

"We must therefore bear" what he regards as "the undoubt-edly bad effects of the weak surviving and propagating their kind." Could any doctrine be more destructive of civiliza-tion? And what a commentary on evolution! He wants us to believe that evolution develops a human sympathy that fi-nally becomes so tender that it repudiates the law that cre-ated it and thus invites a return to a level where the extin-guishing of pity and sympathy will permit the brutal instincts to again do their progressive (?) work. . . .

And what else but the spirit of evolution can account for the popularity of the selfish doctrine, "Each one for himself, and the devil take the hindmost," that threatens the very ex-istence of the doctrine of brotherhood.

In 1900—twenty-five years ago—while an international peace congress was in session in Paris, the following editor-ial appeared in L'Univers:

> The spirit of peace has fled the earth because evolution has taken possession of it. The plea for peace in past years has been inspired by faith in the divine nature and the divine origin of man; men were then looked upon as children of one Father, and war, therefore, was fratricide. But now that men are looked upon as children of apes, what matters it whether they are slaughtered or not?

When there is poison in the blood, no one knows on what part of the body it will break out, but we can be sure that it will continue to break out until the blood is purified. One of the leading universities of the South (I love the state too well to mention its name) publishes a monthly maga-zine entitled "Journal of Social Forces." In the January issue of this year, a contributor has a lengthy article on "Sociol-ogy and Ethics," in the course of which he says:

> No attempt will be made to take up the matter of the good or evil of sexual intercourse among humans aside from the matter of conscious procreation, but as an historian, it might be worth while to ask the exponents of the impurity complex

to explain the fact that, without exception, the great periods of cultural efflorescence have been those characterized by a large amount of freedom in sex-relations, and that those of the greatest cultural degradation and decline have been accompanied with greater sex repression and purity.

No one charges or suspects that all or any large percentage of the advocates of evolution sympathize with this loathsome application of evolution to social life, but it is worthwhile to inquire why those in charge of a great institution of learning allow such filth to be poured out for the stirring of the passions of its students.

Just one more quotation: The Southeastern Christian Advocate of June 25, 1925, quotes five eminent college men of Great Britain as joining in an answer to the question, "Will civilization survive?" Their reply is that:

> The greatest danger menacing our civilization is the abuse of the achievements of science. Mastery over the forces of nature has endowed the twentieth century man with a power which he is not fit to exercise. Unless the development of morality catches up with the development of technique, humanity is bound to destroy itself.

Can any Christian remain indifferent? Science needs religion to direct its energies and to inspire with lofty purpose those who employ the forces that are unloosened by science. Evolution is at war with religion because religion is supernatural; it is, therefore, the relentless foe of Christianity, which is a revealed religion.

Science Needs the Moral Guidance of Religion

Let us, then, hear the conclusion of the whole matter. Science is a magnificent material force, but it is not a teacher of morals. It can perfect machinery, but it adds no moral restraints to protect society from the misuse of the machine. It can also build gigantic intellectual ships, but it constructs no moral rudders for the control of storm-tossed human vessels. It not only fails to supply the spiritual element needed but some of its unproven hypotheses rob the ship of its compass and thus endangers its cargo.

In war, science has proven itself an evil genius; it has made war more terrible than it ever was before. Man used to be content to slaughter his fellowmen on a single plane—the earth's surface. Science has taught him to go down into the water and shoot up from below and to go up into the clouds and shoot down from above, thus making the battlefield three times as bloody as it was before; but science does not teach brotherly love. Science has made war so hellish that civilization was about to commit suicide; and now we are told that newly discovered instruments of destruction will make the cruelties of the late war seem trivial in comparison with the cruelties of wars that may come in the future. If civilization is to be saved from the wreckage threatened by intelligence not consecrated by love, it must be saved by the moral code of the meek and lowly Nazarene. His teachings, and His teachings, alone, can solve the problems that vex the heart and perplex the world.

"The world needs a Savior more than it ever did before, and there is only one Name under heaven given among men whereby we must be saved." It is this Name that evolution degrades, for, carried to its logical conclusion, it robs Christ of the glory of a virgin birth, of the majesty of His deity and mission and of the triumph of His resurrection. It also disputes the doctrine of the atonement.

It is for the jury to determine whether this attack upon the Christian religion shall be permitted in the public schools of Tennessee by teachers employed by the state and paid out of the public treasury. This case is no longer local, the defendant ceases to play an important part. The case has assumed the proportions of a battle-royal between unbelief that attempts to speak through so-called science and the defenders of the Christian faith, speaking through the legislators of Tennessee. It is again a choice between God and Baal; it is also a renewal of the issue in Pilate's court. In that historic trial—the greatest in history—force, impersonated by Pilate occupied the throne. Behind it was the Roman government, mistress of the world, and behind the Roman government were the legions of Rome. Before Pilate, stood Christ, the Apostle of Love. Force triumphed; they nailed Him to the tree and those who stood around mocked and jeered and said, "He is dead." But from that day the power of Caesar waned and the power of Christ increased. In a few centuries the Roman government was gone and its legions forgotten; while the crucified Lord has become the greatest fact in history and the growing figure of all time.

Again force and love meet face to face, and the question, "What shall I do with Jesus?" must be answered. A bloody, brutal doctrine—Evolution—demands, as the rabble did nineteen hundred years ago, that He be crucified. That cannot be the answer of this jury representing a Christian state and sworn to uphold the laws of Tennessee. Your answer will be heard throughout the world; it is eagerly awaited by a praying multitude. If the law is nullified, there will be rejoicing wherever God is repudiated, the Savior scoffed at and the Bible ridiculed. Every unbeliever of every kind and degree will be happy. If, on the other hand, the law is upheld and the religion of the school children protected, millions of Christians will call you blessed and, with hearts full of gratitude to God, will sing again that grand old song of triumph:

Faith of our fathers, living still, In spite of dungeon, fire and sword; O how our hearts beat high with joy Whene'er we hear that glorious word—Faith of our fathers—holy faith; We will be true to thee till death!

Chapter 2

Fact or Fiction?

Evidence in
Support of
Evolution

The Natural World Provides Evidence of Evolution

Charles Darwin

Charles Darwin was the son of a wealthy physician in nineteenth-century England. He was an avid naturalist and a respected member of the scientific community. In his time the study of the natural world was considered a gentleman's hobby, and Darwin never made his living as a scientist. However, he inherited enough money to be able to live quietly in the country, where he could pursue his studies and try to avoid the controversies that his theories provoked.

In 1858 Darwin proposed an alternative explanation for the complexity and order of the natural world. He theorized that competition for scarce resources would tend to weed out more poorly adapted organisms, leaving better adapted organisms to reproduce and pass along their characteristics. Darwin argued that over a long period of time this process, called "natural selection," could account for the complexity and order that is now observed. Darwin's theory replaced

Charles Darwin, *The Origin of Species by Means of Natural Selection, or the Preservation of Favored Races in the Struggle for Life*, John Murray, 1859.

God with an entirely natural mechanism capable of acting without intelligent direction, purpose, or design.

In this passage, from *The Origin of Species*, Darwin argues that the slow process of natural selection explains numerous facts, including the fact that organisms can be classified into related groups, the existence of vestigial organs (webbed feet on geese that do not swim; eyes on fish that cannot see, etc.), the geographical distribution of species, and the geological distribution of fossils. According to Darwin, these facts make perfect sense if they are due to the process of natural selection, but they make no sense at all if we assume that species were created by God.

Under domestication [of animals and plants] we see much variability. This seems to be mainly due to the reproductive system being eminently susceptible to changes in the conditions of life; so that this system, when not rendered impotent, fails to reproduce offspring exactly like the parent-form. Variability is governed by many complex laws,—by correlation of growth, by use and disuse, and by the direct action of the physical conditions of life. There is much difficulty in ascertaining how much modification our domestic productions have undergone; but we may safely infer that the amount has been large, and that modifications can be inherited for long periods. As long as the conditions of life remain the same, we have reason to believe that a modification, which has already been inherited for many generations, may continue to be inherited for an almost infinite number of generations. On the other hand we have evidence that variability, when it has once come into play, does not wholly cease; for new varieties are still occasionally produced by our most anciently domesticated productions.

The Theory of Natural Selection

Man does not actually produce variability; he only unintentionally exposes organic beings to new conditions of life, and then nature acts on the organisation, and causes variability. But man can and does select the variations given to him by nature, and thus accumulate them in any desired manner. He thus adapts animals and plants for his own benefit or pleasure. He may do this methodically, or he may do it unconsciously by preserving the individuals most useful to him at the time, without any thought of altering the breed. It is certain that he can largely influence the character of a breed by selecting, in each successive generation, individual differences so slight as to be quite inappreciable by an uneducated eye. This process of selection has been the great agency in the production of the most distinct and useful domestic breeds. That many of the breeds produced by man have to a large extent the character of natural species, is shown by the inextricable doubts whether very many of them are varieties or aboriginal species.

There is no obvious reason why the principles which have acted so efficiently under domestication should not have acted under nature. In the preservation of favoured individuals and races, during the constantly-recurrent Struggle for Existence, we see the most powerful and ever-acting means of selection. The struggle for existence inevitably follows from the high geometrical ratio of increase which is common to all organic beings. This high rate of increase is proved by calculation, by the effects of a succession of peculiar seasons, and by the results of naturalisation. More individuals are born than can possibly survive. A grain in the balance will determine which individual shall live and which shall die,—which variety or species shall increase in number, and which shall decrease, or finally become extinct. As the individuals of the same species come in all respects into the closest competition with each other, the struggle will generally be most severe between them; it will be almost equally severe between the varieties of the same species, and next in severity between the species of the same genus. But the struggle will often be very severe between beings most remote in the scale of nature. The slightest advantage in one being, at any age or during any season, over those with which it comes into competition, or better adaptation in however slight a degree to the surrounding physical conditions, will turn the balance.

With animals having separated sexes there will in most cases be a struggle between the males for possession of the females. The most vigorous individuals, or those which have most successfully struggled with their conditions of life, will generally leave most progeny. But success will often depend on having special weapons or means of defence, or on the charms of the males; and the slightest advantage will lead to victory.

As geology plainly proclaims that each land has undergone great physical changes, we might have expected that organic beings would have varied under nature, in the same way as they generally have varied under the changed conditions of domestication. And if there be any variability under nature, it would be an unaccountable fact if natural selection had not come into play. It has often been asserted, but the assertion is quite incapable of proof, that the amount of variation under nature is a strictly limited quantity. Man, though acting on external characters alone and often capriciously, can produce within a short period a great result by adding up mere individual differences in his domestic productions; and every one admits that there are at least individual differences in species under nature. But, besides such differences, all naturalists have admitted the existence of varieties, which they think sufficiently distinct to be worthy of record in systematic works. No one can draw any clear distinction between individual differences and slight varieties; or between more plainly marked varieties and subspecies, and species. Let it be observed how naturalists differ in the rank which they assign to the many representative forms in Europe and North America.

If then we have under nature variability and a powerful agent always ready to act and select, why should we doubt that variations in any way useful to beings, under their excessively complex relations of life, would be preserved, accumulated, and inherited? Why, if man can by patience select variations most useful to himself, should nature fail in selecting variations useful, under changing conditions of life, to her living products? What limit can be put to this power, acting during long ages and rigidly scrutinising the whole constitution, structure, and habits of each creature,— favouring the good and rejecting the bad? I can see no limit to this power, in slowly and beautifully adapting each form to the most complex relations of life. The theory of natural selection, even if we looked no further than this, seems to me to be in itself probable. I have already recapitulated, as fairly as I could, the opposed difficulties and objections: now let us turn to the special facts and arguments in favour of the theory.

Evidence Based on Classification of Species

On the view that species are only strongly marked and permanent varieties, and that each species first existed as a variety, we can see why it is that no line of demarcation can be drawn between species, commonly supposed to have been produced by special acts of creation, and varieties which are acknowledged to have been produced by secondary laws. On this same view we can understand how it is that in each region where many species of a genus have been produced, and where they now flourish, these same species should present many varieties; for where the manufactory of species has been active, we might expect, as a general rule, to find it still in action; and this is the case if varieties be incipient species. Moreover, the species of the large genera, which afford the greater number of varieties or incipient species, retain to a certain degree the character of varieties; for they differ from each other by a less amount of difference than do the species of smaller genera. The closely allied species also of the larger genera apparently have restricted ranges, and they are clustered in little groups round other species—in which respects they resemble varieties. These are strange relations on the view of each species having been independently created, but are intelligible if all species first existed as varieties.

As each species tends by its geometrical ratio of reproduction to increase inordinately in number; and as the modified descendants of each species will be enabled to increase by so much the more as they become more diversified in habits and structure, so as to be enabled to seize on many and widely different places in the economy of nature, there will be a constant tendency in natural selection to preserve the most divergent offspring of any one species. Hence during a long-continued course of modification, the slight differences, characteristic of varieties of the same species, tend to be augmented into the greater differences characteristic of species of the same genus. New and improved varieties will inevitably supplant and exterminate the older, less improved and intermediate varieties; and thus species are rendered to a large extent defined and distinct objects. Dominant species belonging to the larger groups tend to give birth to new and dominant forms; so that each large group tends to become still larger, and at the same time more divergent in character. But as all groups cannot thus succeed in increasing in size, for the world would not hold them, the more dominant groups beat the less dominant. This tendency in the large groups to go on increasing in size and diverging in character, together with the almost inevitable contingency of much extinction, explains the arrangement of all the forms of life, in groups subordinate to groups, all within a few great classes, which we now see everywhere around us, and which has prevailed throughout all time. This grand fact of the grouping of all organic beings seems to me utterly inexplicable on the theory of creation.

As natural selection acts solely by accumulating slight, successive, favourable variations, it can produce no great or sudden modification; it can act only by very short and slow steps. Hence the canon of 'Natura non facit saltum,' which every fresh addition to our knowledge tends to make more strictly correct, is on this theory simply intelligible. We can plainly see why nature is prodigal in variety, though niggard in innovation. But why this should be a law of nature if each species has been independently created, no man can explain.

Evidence Based on Curiosities of Nature

Many other facts are, as it seems to me, explicable on this theory. How strange it is that a bird, under the form of woodpecker, should have been created to prey on insects on the ground; that upland geese, which never or rarely swim, should have been created with webbed feet; that a thrush should have been created to dive and feed on sub-aquatic insects; and that a petrel should have been created with habits and structure fitting it for the life of an auk or grebe! and so on in endless other cases. But on the view of each species constantly trying to increase in number, with natural selection always ready to adapt the slowly varying descendants of each to any unoccupied or ill-occupied place in nature, these facts cease to be strange, or perhaps might even have been anticipated.

As natural selection acts by competition, it adapts the inhabitants of each country only in relation to the degree of perfection of their associates; so that we need feel no surprise at the inhabitants of any one country, although on the ordinary view supposed to have been specially created and adapted for that country, being beaten and supplanted by the naturalised productions from another land. Nor ought we to marvel if all the contrivances in nature be not, as far as we can judge, absolutely perfect; and if some of them be abhorrent to our ideas of fitness. We need not marvel at the sting of the bee causing the bee's own death; at drones being produced in such vast numbers for one single act, and being then slaughtered by their sterile sisters; at the astonishing waste of pollen by our fir-trees; at the instinctive hatred of the queen bee for her own fertile daughters; at ichneumonidae feeding within the live bodies of caterpillars; and at other such cases. The wonder indeed is, on the theory of natural selection, that more cases of the want of absolute perfection have not been observed.

The complex and little known laws governing variation are the same, as far as we can see, with the laws which have governed the production of so-called specific forms. In both cases physical conditions seem to have produced but little direct effect; yet when varieties enter any zone, they occasionally assume some of the characters of the species proper to that zone. In both varieties and species, use and disuse seem to have produced some effect; for it is difficult to resist this conclusion when we look, for instance, at the logger-headed duck, which has wings incapable of flight, in nearly the same condition as in the domestic duck; or when we look at the burrowing tucutucu, which is occasionally blind, and then at certain moles, which are habitually blind and have their eyes covered with skin; or when we look at the blind animals inhabiting the dark caves of America and Europe. In both varieties and species correction of growth seems to have played a most important part, so that when one part has been modified other parts are necessarily modified. In both varieties and species reversions to long-lost characters occur. How inexplicable on the theory of creation is the occasional appearance of stripes on the shoulder and legs of the several species of the horse-genus and in their hybrids! How simply is this fact explained if we believe that these species have descended from a striped progenitor, in the same manner as the several domestic breeds of pigeon have descended from the blue and barred rock-pigeon!

On the ordinary view of each species having been independently created, why should the specific characters, or those by which the species of the same genus differ from each other, be more variable than the generic characters in which they all agree? Why, for instance, should the colour of a flower be more likely to vary in any one species of a genus, if the other species, supposed to have been created independently, have differently coloured flowers, than if all the species of the genus have the same coloured flowers? If species are only well-marked varieties, of which the characters have become in a high degree permanent, we can understand this fact; for they have already varied since they branched off from a common progenitor in certain characters, by which they have come to be specifically distinct from each other; and therefore these same characters would be more likely still to be variable than the generic characters which have been inherited without change for an enormous period. It is inexplicable on the theory of creation why a part developed in a very unusual manner in any one species of a genus, and therefore, as we may naturally infer, of great importance to the species, should be eminently liable to variation; but, on my view, this part has undergone, since the several species branched off from a common progenitor, an unusual amount of variability and modification, and therefore we might expect this part generally to be still variable. But a part may be developed in the most unusual manner, like the wing of a bat, and yet not be more variable than any other structure, if the part be common to many subordinate forms, that is, if it has been inherited for a very long period; for in this case it will have been rendered constant by long-continued natural selection.

Glancing at instincts, marvellous as some are, they offer no greater difficulty than does corporeal structure on the theory of the natural selection of successive, slight, but profitable modifications. We can thus understand why nature moves by graduated steps in endowing different animals of the same class with their several instincts. I have attempted to show how much light the principle of gradation throws on the admirable architectural powers of the hive-bee. Habit no doubt sometimes comes into play in modifying instincts; but it certainly is not indispensable, as we see, in the case of neuter insects, which leave no progeny to inherit the effects of long-continued habit. On the view of all the species of the same genus having descended from a common parent, and having inherited much in common, we can understand how it is that allied species, when placed under considerably different conditions of life, yet should follow nearly the same instincts; why the thrush of South America, for instance, lines her nest with mud like our British species. On the view of instincts having been slowly acquired through natural selection we need not marvel at some instincts being apparently not perfect and liable to mistakes, and at many instincts causing other animals to suffer.

If species be only well-marked and permanent varieties, we can at once see why their crossed offspring should follow the same complex laws in their degrees and kinds of resemblance to their parents,—in being absorbed into each other by successive crosses, and in other such points,—as do the crossed offspring of acknowledged varieties. On the other hand, these would be strange facts if species have been independently created, and varieties have been produced by secondary laws.

Evidence Based on Geology and Geography

If we admit that the geological record is imperfect in an extreme degree, then such facts as the record gives, support the theory of descent with modification. New species have come on the stage slowly and at successive intervals; and the amount of change, after equal intervals of time, is widely different in different groups. The extinction of species and of whole groups of species, which has played so conspicuous a part in the history of the organic world, almost inevitably follows on the principle of natural selection; for old forms will be supplanted by new and improved forms. Neither single species nor groups of species reappear when the chain of ordinary generation has once been broken. The gradual diffusion of dominant forms, with the slow modification of their descendants, causes the forms of life, after long intervals of time, to appear as if they had changed simultaneously throughout the world. The fact of the fossil remains of each formation being in some degree intermediate in character between the fossils in the formations above and below, is simply explained by their intermediate position in the chain of descent. The grand fact that all extinct organic beings belong to the same system with recent beings, falling either into the same or into intermediate groups, follows from the living and the extinct being the offspring of common parents. As the groups which have descended from an ancient progenitor have generally diverged in character, the progenitor with its early descendants will often be intermediate in character in comparison with its later descendants; and thus we can see why the more ancient a fossil is, the oftener it stands in some degree intermediate between existing and allied groups. Recent forms are generally looked at as being, in some vague sense, higher than ancient and extinct forms; and they are in so far higher as the later and more improved forms have conquered the older and less improved organic beings in the struggle for life. Lastly, the law of the long endurance of allied forms on the same continent,—of marsupials in Australia, of edentata in America, and other such cases,—is intelligible, for within a confined country, the recent and the extinct will naturally be allied by descent.

Looking to geographical distribution, if we admit that there has been during the long course of ages much migration from one part of the world to another, owing to former climatal and geographical changes and to the many occasional and unknown means of dispersal, then we can understand, on the theory of descent with modification, most of the great leading facts in Distribution. We can see why there should be so striking a parallelism in the distribution of organic beings throughout space, and in their geological succession throughout time; for in both cases the beings have been connected by the bond of ordinary generation, and the means of modification have been the same. We see the full meaning of the wonderful fact, which must have struck every traveller, namely, that on the same continent, under the most diverse conditions, under heat and cold, on mountain and lowland, on deserts and marshes, most of the inhabitants within each great class are plainly related; for they will generally be descendants of the same progenitors and early colonists. On this same principle of former migration, combined in most cases with modification, we

can understand, by the aid of the Glacial period, the iden-
tity of some few plants, and the close alliance of many others, on the most distant mountains, under the most different climates; and likewise the close alliance of some of the
inhabitants of the sea in the northern and southern tem-
perate zones, though separated by the whole intertropical
ocean. Although two areas may present the same physical
conditions of life, we need feel no surprise at their inhabitants being widely different, if they have been for a long period completely separated from each other; for as the relation of organism to organism is the most important of all
relations, and as the two areas will have received colonists
from some third source or from each other, at various periods and in different proportions, the course of modification
in the two areas will inevitably be different.

On this view of migration, with subsequent modification, we can see why oceanic islands should be inhabited by
few species, but of these, that many should be peculiar. We
can clearly see why those animals which cannot cross wide
spaces of ocean, as frogs and terrestrial mammals, should
not inhabit oceanic islands; and why, on the other hand,
new and peculiar species of bats, which can traverse the
ocean, should so often be found on islands far distant from
any continent. Such facts as the presence of peculiar species
of bats, and the absence of all other mammals, on oceanic
islands, are utterly inexplicable on the theory of independent acts of creation.

The existence of closely allied or representative species in
any two areas, implies, on the theory of descent with modification, that the same parents formerly inhabited both areas; and we almost invariably find that wherever many
closely allied species inhabit two areas, some identical
species common to both still exist. Wherever many closely
allied yet distinct species occur, many doubtful forms and

varieties of the same species likewise occur. It is a rule of high generality that the inhabitants of each area are related to the inhabitants of the nearest source whence immigrants might have been derived. We see this in nearly all the plants and animals of the Galapagos archipelago, of Juan Fernandez, and of the other American islands being related in the most striking manner to the plants and animals of the neighbouring American mainland; and those of the Cape de Verde archipelago and other African islands to the African mainland. It must be admitted that these facts receive no explanation on the theory of creation.

The Earth Is Very Old

Tim M. Berra

Creationists often attack the claim that the earth is known to be 4.5 billion years old. Some argue that the earth was created as recently as six thousand years ago, and they question the radiometric dating methods used by scientists to come up with the 4.5-billion-year estimate.

In this selection Tim M. Berra contradicts the claim by creationists that radiometric dating methods are likely to be mistaken. Radioactive decay, he says, proceeds at an "utterly constant rate," and the measurements have been performed thousands of times by many different scientists. The age of the earth has been established beyond all reasonable doubt.

Berra received his Ph.D. in biology from Tulane University. He is a two-time recipient of the Fulbright Fellowship. Currently he holds the position of professor emeritus at Ohio State University in the Department of Evolution, Ecology, and Organismal Biology. He is the author of five books and over fifty peer-reviewed papers.

Tim M. Berra, *Evolution and the Myth of Creationism: A Basic Guide to the Facts in the Evolution Debate*. Stanford, CA: Stanford University Press, 1990. Copyright © 1990 by the Board of Trustees of the Leland Stanford Junior University. Reprinted by permission.

Until well into this century, geologists and paleontologists had to be content with a knowledge of the *relative* age of a rock stratum; it was older than this one, younger than that one, and the fossils it contained allowed scientists to relate its age to other rock in other parts of the world. But how old it might really be, or the Earth itself might be, could not be determined by any scientific means then available. Today, however, we are able to determine the *absolute* age of ancient rocks, whether they contain fossils or not, by means of a technique called radiometric dating. All rocks are composed of minerals, and many minerals contain a radioactive isotope (radioisotope) of an element such as uranium that acts as a natural clock. One by one, at an absolutely predictable rate, the radioactive atoms of a radioisotope spontaneously decay (break down) into atoms of a new, nonradioactive material. Because of this constant decay, the radioisotope is said to be unstable; it changes over time. What it changes to, called the disintegration product, is a different element, stable forever in its composition. The decay of the radioisotope continues over vast periods of time, but at a fixed rate, independent of temperature, pressure, or other environmental variables. *No other process on Earth proceeds at such an utterly constant rate.*

Half-Life

The decay rate that is so dependable in the absolute dating of rocks is expressed as the half-life of the radioisotope; that is the time it takes for half of the radioactive atoms in the sample to decay. For example, let's say that unstable isotope A decays to stable isotope B with a half-life of 1,000,000 years. If we start with 1,000 atoms of A, then at the end of

1,000,000 years, we will have 500 atoms of A and 500 atoms of B. At the end of 2,000,000 years, half of the remaining atoms of A would have decayed, and we would be left with 250 atoms of A and 750 atoms of B, and so on. If we are given a sample of a rock, and we find that it contains 125 atoms of A and 875 atoms of B, then we can determine quite directly that the rock was formed 3,000,000 years ago. All we need is some means of accurately counting the atoms of A and the atoms of B, for if we know the half-life of a radioisotope, and can measure the amount of the radioactive element remaining and the amount of the disintegration product present, we can back-calculate to the time the sample was originally formed, when none of it had begun to decay.

Today, science has such a means. Several radioactive isotopes are used in determining geologic time. A mass number (the sum of the protons and neutrons in the nucleus of an atom) designates each isotope. Thus we have uranium 238, which decays to lead 206 with a half-life of 4.5 billion years. Uranium 235 decays to lead 207 with a half-life of 704 million years. Potassium 40 decays to argon 40 with a half-life of 1.25 billion years. The potassium-argon system is relatively common in rocks and is therefore more widely used than other systems. Each of these decay processes (there are several others, as well) offers us a system of dating, and in each case the extent of the decay can be measured in the laboratory with great precision. The use of more than one of these systems on a given rock sample helps ensure the accuracy of the dating. (Still, if knowing the rock's age is to be of any value, it is crucial that the geologist has recorded precisely where the rock sample was taken from the ground.)

The theory of radiometric dating is very simple, but in practice the technique is complicated by difficulties in making precise measurements of tiny amounts of isotopes. Moreover, not all rocks can be used for radiometric dating. Igneous rocks (rocks that cooled from the molten state), such as volcanic or granitic rocks, are the best for radiometric dating. Fossils do not occur in such rocks, but if fossils occur *between* two undisturbed layers of volcanic rock, the age of the fossils has to be between the dates of the two volcanic strata. Some skeletons, if they have incorporated sufficient amounts of uranium, may be dated directly. Measurements of the decay of uranium 235 to lead 207, even in very small samples of fossils, are accurate to within 2 percent, but 2 percent of a billion years is a lot of time, and a corroboration from stratigraphy can be valuable.

Radiocarbon (carbon 14) dating can be applied directly to fossils or organic human artifacts (but not stone artifacts) and can be quite accurate. Unstable carbon 14 is formed in the atmosphere from stable nitrogen 14 by the bombardment of cosmic rays from space. Because its rate of formation balances its rate of decay, in atmospheric carbon dioxide the proportion of unstable carbon (^{14}C) relative to ordinary carbon (^{12}C) is essentially constant. Plants take in the atmospheric carbon dioxide from the air, and animals eat the plants. Thus both plants and animals have a fixed amount of ^{14}C in their tissues while alive, but after death no new ^{14}C can replace the amount lost by radioactive decay to ^{14}N. Therefore, by measuring the remaining proportion of ^{14}C relative to ^{12}C, we can calculate the approximate time of death as far back as about 50,000 years ago. In a sample older than that, the amount of ^{14}C remaining today is too small to be accurately measured (the half-life of ^{14}C is just 5,730 years). Creationists attempt to discredit ^{14}C dating by applying it to fossils older than 50,000 years, or in other inappropriate ways, and then showing that it yields obviously erroneous dates.

How Old Is the Earth?

By combining the results of the absolute dating method (calculating radioactive decay) with those of the relative dating method (seeing what rock strata lie above and below), we can interpret the fossil record with increasing confidence. *The age of the Earth and Moon has been demonstrated to be about 4.5 billion years.* This is not a guess based upon a few selected rocks. Over the last 30 years nearly 100 independent laboratories worldwide have published in the scientific literature over 100,000 radiometric ages that support this conclusion.

The earliest fossils discovered to date are bacteria and primitive plants called blue-green algae, which date back to about 3.5 billion years. Other Precambrian fossils include sponge spicules and impressions of jellyfish, soft corals, and segmented worms. We are lucky to have any fossils this old, because rocks of such antiquity have been greatly folded and distorted, and because the earliest animals were mostly soft-bodied, with few hard parts to fossilize. Cambrian rocks, however, from 570 million years ago (MYA), are rich with the remains of many invertebrate groups, such as protozoans, sponges, jellyfish, and various shelled organisms.

As one moves forward in geologic time, up into higher rock strata, other groups of animals are encountered. The first known backboned animals, primitive fishes called ostracoderms, appeared in the late Cambrian, over 500 MYA, the first jawed fishes (placoderms) in the Silurian, the first amphibians in the Devonian, the first reptiles in the Carboniferous. The Mesozoic is known as the "Age of Reptiles" for its proliferation of dinosaurs and other reptiles. The first known mammals and birds split away from different reptilian ancestors in the Triassic and Jurassic, respectively. Primates, the mammalian order to which we belong, arose in the Paleocene and were widespread by the Oligocene, about 38 MYA.

This sequential appearance of different groups at different times, the more advanced appearing in general later than the more primitive, is predicted by evolutionary theory. *It cannot be reconciled with creationism,* which requires all groups to have come into existence essentially simultaneously and fully formed a mere 6,000 to 10,000 years ago. People once thought that the Earth was flat and that it was the center of the universe. It is now high time we laid the creationist ideas to rest, as well.

The Story of Noah's Flood Cannot Explain the Facts of Natural History

Chris McGowan

Many modern creationists not only expect the creation stories of the Bible to be accurate descriptions of the origin of life, they also expect the story of Noah's flood to be an accurate description of the destruction of species now known to be extinct. Taken literally, the story of Noah's flood offers many specific facts that could potentially be verified (or falsified) by calculations based on current knowledge.

Chris McGowan is a vertebrate zoologist at the University of Toronto. His primary research interest is the extinct group of marine reptiles known as ichthyosaurs, and he has written a book, *The Dragon Seekers*, about the early fossil hunters who first discovered ichthyosaurs, plesiosaurs, and other Mesozoic marine reptiles.

Chris McGowan, *In the Beginning . . . A Scientist Shows Why the Creationists Are Wrong*. Amherst, NY: Prometheus Books, 1984. Copyright © 1984 Chris McGowan. Reprinted by permission of the publisher.

In this selection McGowan calculates the capacity of the Ark and concludes, based on very generous assumptions, that the Ark might have been able to hold the necessary numbers of land animals, but would not have been able to hold enough food to keep them alive during the voyage and that Noah would also have had to rescue salt-water species of fish from seas diluted by fresh rain. Finally, he argues that a migration from Mt. Ararat following the voyage would have been impossible for most species, since they would have been outside their required habitat and would have died before reaching their current locations. He concludes that the story cannot be taken literally.

I find it hard to believe that anyone could accept a literal interpretation of the Noachian flood. I find it equally hard to believe that I should be sitting at my desk in 1982 documenting the reasons why the flood could not have happened according to Genesis. The fact remains, though, that a large number of people do believe that a worldwide flood destroyed all living things on the earth, save those that were taken aboard the ark. These same people believe that fossils are the remains of those organisms that perished in the flood, and that their relative position in the rocks is largely a result of where they were living when they were overcome by the flood. If people want to accept the story of the ark on faith, I have no wish to take issue with them. However, if they tell me that they have scientific evidence to support their belief, as Dr. [Henry M.] Morris does, it is an entirely different matter. Dr. Morris tells us that

> If the system of flood geology can be established on a sound scientific basis, and be effectively promoted and publicized, then the entire evolutionary cosmology, at least in its pre-

sent neo-Darwinian form, will collapse. This, in turn, would mean that every anti-Christian system and movement (communism, racism, humanism, libertinism, behaviorism, and all the rest) would be deprived of their pseudo-intellectual foundation.

After firing this broadside against anti-Christians, a term which he broadly interprets as all those who are not creationists, Dr. Morris gives us a few facts about the flood:

- The flood was worldwide and, since the ark came to rest on Mount Ararat (Genesis 8:4), the waters were at least 5000 m deep (about 3 miles) based on the present elevation of Mount Ararat.
- The flood lasted for a little more than ten months (after the forty days and nights of rain).
- The ark had a capacity at least equivalent to 522 standard railway stock cars. This, according to Dr. Morris, is more than twice the volume required to accommodate two of every species of land animal that ever lived.
- The flood destroyed everything; it "overturned the earth."

Before we examine the plausibility of these points, we should add two more pieces of information from Genesis that Dr. Morris has omitted.

- Noah was instructed to take seven of every clean beast (animals with a cloven hoof that chew the cud, that is, ruminants) and seven of every bird, as well as two of every other kind of animal. (Genesis 7:2–3)
- Noah was instructed to take enough food for all the animals, as well as for his own family. (Genesis 6:21)

We should also add that although Noah was not instructed to take marine organisms aboard the ark, the fact remains that most of these, from sea anemones and corals to sharks and whales, are unable to tolerate fresh water. If the forty days and nights of rain covered the earth with 5000 m of water, it follows that most marine organisms would have perished, unless they were taken into the ark. (The creationists might argue that the waters from the "fountains of the great deep" maintained the salinity of the sea, but this explanation strays beyond the bounds of science.)

The first and obvious question is whether the ark could have carried all of its occupants. According to Genesis 6:15, the ark was 300 cubits long by 50 cubits wide and 30 cubits high. A cubit is about 44 cm; therefore the dimensions of the ark were approximately 150 m × 25 m × 15 m, which is an overestimate (I am intentionally erring on the side of the creationists). The maximum capacity was therefore 56 250 cubic meters, which is again an overestimate because it does not allow for the fact that the ark would have been boat-shaped and not rectilinear, or for the space taken up by the walls that Noah was instructed to build (Genesis 6:14), or for any of the superstructure and decking, or for the barriers and cages that would have been required to keep the various animals apart. The available space would have been considerably less than 56 250 cubic meters.

There are over one million species of animals living today, together with about half a million plant species (the latter could, of course, for the most part have been taken along as seeds). Although the exercise is rather simplistic, let us now divide the 56 250 cubic meters of space, which we know to be a gross overestimate, by the 1.12 million number of animal species to see how much room each species could occupy. The result is 0.05 cubic meters, which is about one-third of the capacity of a domestic oven. Now this is more than enough space for a pair of ants or a pair of mice but it is rather inadequate for a pair of squirrels, and quite out of the question for a pair of zebra. However, we have to bear in mind that most animals are smaller than zebras; insects, after all, account for about seventy-five percent of the total number of species, and most of these could live in a space of 0.05 cubic meters quite happily. If we therefore allocated the space according to the size of the animals, we might conceivably pack them all into the space, but we have to remember that this space is not available space, merely the volume of the ark. It is therefore most unlikely that the ark could have held all the animals.

Food and Water

What about the food for the journey? . . . Warm-blooded animals consume large quantities of food. An African elephant, for example, eats about 160 kg of fodder a day, so that a pair of them would consume about 96 metric tonnes during the voyage. Now 96 tonnes of hay occupies a considerable amount of space when you consider that a standard bale weighs about 32 kg. Just imagine how much hay would be needed for all the other pairs of ungulates—hippo, tapir, zebra, warthog, llama, boar, peccary, ass, camel, chevrotain, horse, to mention only a few. But we have forgotten something: the ruminants were not in pairs but in sevens—seven pronghorns, seven bison, seven muskox, seven ibex, seven moose, seven sheep, seven wapiti, seven goat, seven gazelle, seven eland, seven wildebeest, seven oryx, seven impala, seven reindeer . . . They would eat an awful lot of hay in three hundred days, and think of all the fertilizer Noah would have to shovel away. Then there are all those carnivores to worry about. A lion, for example, consumes its own weight in food every eight or nine days, so that a pair of lions would eat about 35 kg of meat a day. This would amount to some 10 tonnes during the voyage, and what about all the other pairs of carnivores? Aside from the space problem of storing many hundreds of tonnes of meat, there is the problem of keeping it fresh. Remember that this was before the days of refrigerators. I suppose the meat could have been salted, but I am not sure whether carnivores will eat salt meat, and if they did, it would make them very thirsty. Now this raises another problem.

We have touched upon the problem of food storage but have said nothing about fresh water. Would the flood waters have been drinkable with all those dead things floating around in it, or would Noah have had to provision the ark with water? If fresh drinking-water had to be carried, this would have presented horrendous storage problems.

What about the birds? There are over 8000 species, and Noah was told to take along seven of each kind. Fifty-six thousand birds would eat their way through a mountain of food during the voyage. There is also the problem of animals with special diets. Koala bears, for example, will only eat eucalyptus leaves, and these have to be supplied fresh every day. I can see no alternatives but having eucalyptus trees growing on board.

And what about the special requirements for the marine organisms? Just consider how many watertight containers would be required to keep all the various sea creatures in. Imagine how large a tank would be required for just one species of whale, let alone for all the others. The sharks would need a big tank, too, and so would the seals, and the sea lions and the walruses, and the squids and the octopuses, and all the other large animals that live in the sea. And they would have to have been kept separate from each other; otherwise they would have started eating one another. There is also the problem of keeping the sea water clean and healthy; not an easy task, as anyone who has tried to keep a marine aquarium knows.

The only way for the creationists to remove the logistics problem of the ark is to argue that if God willed it to be so, then so it was. But this strategy defeats Dr. Morris's wish for the Noachian flood to be "established on a sound scientific basis."

Not only are the packaging and maintenance problems of the ark untenable, but so too is the problem of dispersing the animals and plants to their native lands at the end of the voyage. We are told in Genesis 8:4 that the ark came to rest on the mountains of Ararat. How did all the animals find enough to eat on that mountainside in Turkey when the flood subsided? We are told that everything was destroyed during the flood; it would therefore have taken some time before plants could have started growing again, and these presumably would have to have been sown by Noah. What did the plant-eaters do while they were waiting for the plants to grow? What did the meat-eaters do while they were waiting for the plant-eaters to multiply? Could Noah have had sufficient supplies in that first season? Hardly—we have already shown that he could not have carried anywhere near enough supplies for the original voyage.

Assuming that all the animals managed to survive that difficult period following the flood, which is seemingly impossible, how did they disperse themselves to the four corners of the earth? How did the two pandas make it right across Eurasia to China? How did the two kangaroos hop across Eurasia and then across the ocean to Australia? Are we to suppose that it was not the original Noachian pairs that traveled these enormous distances, but later generations? If that is so, then we have to accept that Turkey and its environs must have been suitable for all the animals and plants; otherwise they would all have perished right there and then. Can you imagine a climate that would have been suitable for tropical and for polar organisms at one and the same time? The story of the ark, quite clearly, cannot stand up to scientific scrutiny. This is hardly surprising, as I do not believe it was ever meant to be taken literally.

Evolution Does Not Violate the Laws of Thermodynamics

Philip Kitcher

Thermodynamics, which began as the study of the movement of heat, is now the branch of physics that studies energy transfers in any context. From the study of thermodynamics comes the concept of entropy, the tendency of order to fall into chaos. The second law of thermodynamics states that any "system" by itself tends to become disordered, that is, less complex. Evolution, however, seems to cause things to become more complex. Hence it appears that evolution violates the second law of thermodynamics.

In this selection, Philip Kitcher explains the apparent contradiction between thermodynamics and evolution, and shows why this appearance of contradiction is mistaken. The second law of thermodynamics is an ideal statement about "closed" systems, and life on earth is not a closed system. Sunlight provides abundant available energy for reversing entropy in this local region of space without violating any laws of physics.

Philip Kitcher, *Abusing Science: The Case Against Creationism*. Cambridge, MA: MIT Press, 1990. Copyright © 1982 by The Massachusetts Institute of Technology. Reproduced by permission.

Philip Kitcher is a professor of philosophy at Columbia University. His chief area of study is philosophy of the sciences, including both mathematics and biology. In addition to *Abusing Science*, from which this selection is taken, his books include *Vaulting Ambition*, a critique of the new science of sociobiology.

Creationists love the laws of thermodynamics. Certainly, these laws are worth celebrating as major achievements of classical physics. Yet we might suspect the rhapsodies in which Creationists indulge: "It is well to note at this point, the implications of the First and Second Laws of Thermodynamics with respect to the origin of the universe. It should be stressed that these two Laws are *proven* scientific laws, if there is such a thing" (creationist Henry M. Morris). Morris and his fellows are not moved to applause by their fine appreciation of thermodynamics and the evidence that corroborates it. Their accolades are intended to tell us which side to choose when we find that evolutionary theory and thermodynamics are in conflict.

The first law of thermodynamics is a principle about energy conservation. In its original form, it asserts that mechanical energy is equivalent to energy in the form of heat. I shall not be concerned here with a more precise statement of the law, nor shall I investigate the arguments, which occasionally appear, suggesting that the first law contradicts evolutionary theory. The reason is that, much as they love the first law, Creationists are even more devoted to the second.

Understanding Entropy

A key concept in the second law of thermodynamics is the concept of entropy. There are various ways to understand entropy. One approach is to take the entropy of a system to be a function of that energy in the system that is unavailable for work. An ordinary engine, such as a steam engine or an internal combustion engine, can exploit only some of the energy stored within it. Some of the stored energy is locked away and unusable. To compute the entropy of the engine is to figure out how much of its internal energy is locked up in this way. The metaphor of locking up energy is easily understood by example. If we have two bodies at different temperatures, the heat energy of the colder body will not spontaneously flow to the warmer, thereby increasing the temperature difference; in this sense the heat energy of the cooler is "locked up." (An alternative way of viewing the entropy of a system is as a measure of the disorder of the system. In addition, the entropy concept can be introduced in terms of information theory. I shall follow the approach of classical thermodynamics, in which entropy is seen as a function of unusable energy. But the points I make will not be affected by this choice.)

The second law of thermodynamics is concerned with *closed* systems. From the thermodynamical view, a system is open if it is exchanging energy with what lies beyond its boundary. Closed systems are those that neither give energy to their environment nor receive energy from it. We may imagine a perfectly insulated box containing objects of various temperatures. Energy is exchanged among the objects in the box; some of them warm up, others cool down. (The hotter objects cool down, the colder warm up, until an equilibrium is reached.) However, there is no energy flow across the surface of the box. This imagined box would constitute a thermodynamically closed system.

We can now state the second law: The entropy of a closed system increases with time. What this means is that if we have a thermodynamically closed system, like our imagined box, the total amount of energy within it remains constant through time, but an increasing proportion of that energy becomes unavailable to do work. (Alternatively, the system becomes even more disordered.) The formulation that I have given accords with those found in textbooks on physics. But it does not coincide with the statements of the second law offered by some Creationists.

Creationists like to present the second law either by omitting any mention of its restriction to closed systems or by choosing a statement that does not make this restriction clear. Consider the following passages:

> The second law of thermodynamics is the law of increasing entropy, stating that all real processes tend to go towards a state of higher probability, which means greater disorder. This law applies to all known systems, both physical and biological, a fact which is universally accepted by scientists in every field. (Morris)

> Basically the second law says three things:

> 1. Systems will tend toward the most probable state.

> 2. Systems will tend toward the most random state.

> 3. Systems will increase entropy, where entropy is a measure of the availability of energy to do useful work. (Creationist Randy L. Wysong)

> The Second Law of Thermodynamics, also universal and invariable beyond any scientific doubt, states that, although the total amount of energy remains unchanged, in all real processes, some of the energy involved (all processes in the universe, be they physical, geological, biological, etc. involve energy transformations) is transformed into non-reversible heat energy and is no longer available for work. (Creationist Henry Hiebert)

In all these cases, Creationists fail to acknowledge that the second law states only that the entropy of *closed* systems increases. Elsewhere, they quote a statement by Isaac Asimov, intended to provide a non-technical explanation of the second law: "'In any physical change that takes place by itself the entropy always increases.' (Entropy is 'a measure of the quantity of energy *not* capable of conversion into work.')" Asimov's statement is not inaccurate. But its reference to closed systems—borne by the phrase "takes place by itself"—is easily overlooked.

Does Evolution Reverse Entropy?

Why is the second law supposed to constitute a problem for evolutionary theory? The basic idea is simple. According to the second law, "There is an inexorable downhill trend toward ultimate complete randomness, utter meaninglessness, and absolute stillness" (Morris). However, *any* Darwinian history presupposes an "upward trend" toward increasing complexity and organization. Faced with the "anti-evolutionary implications of the Second Law of Thermodynamics," evolutionary theorists are supposed to trot out a number of standard desperate responses: The second law "does not apply to living systems"; The law is "a statistical statement" with possible exceptions; The law may not always have operated; and so forth. As an afterthought, evolutionary theory is allowed its most obvious response: The second law applies only to closed systems.

Let us be completely clear about the logic of the situation. Evolutionary theory would contradict the second law if (and *only* if) the construction of Darwinian histories required us to suppose the existence of thermodynamically closed systems in which entropy does not increase. But no such supposition is required. Darwinian histories do presuppose that large amounts of energy remain available for work in large numbers of systems of living things. Let us consider the following kinds of systems: an organism, a genealogy including an initial pair of organisms and their descendants, a lineage consisting of an ancestral population and its descendants, and the total lineage that comprises all life on earth. In many systems of these kinds, entropy *decreases* over time. But the systems in question are all open. Energy from the sun is constantly entering the system comprising the earth and its inhabitants. That energy flows into lesser organic systems as they feed and warm themselves.

Creationists are very vague about exactly where evolutionary theory contradicts the second law. They do not point to some particular feature of Darwinian histories and show that that feature presupposes a system that thermodynamics disallows. However, it may help to dissolve any lingering worries if we look at life on earth from the perspective of classical thermodynamics. Since the earth receives large amounts of energy from the sun, we cannot think of the earth as a closed system. By broadening our horizons, however, we can view the earth as part of a closed system. That closed system will include the earth, the sun, and those regions of the universe that exchange energy with them. (It will be extremely large.) Classical thermodynamics tells us that, within this vast closed system, entropy increases. It says absolutely nothing about entropy variation at the local level. Thus the fact that the system contains pockets in which entropy decreases (for example, the subsystem comprising terrestrial life) is perfectly compatible with the laws of classical thermodynamics.

Unfortunately, this is not the end of the story. Although they do not refer to closed systems in stating the second law, Creationists have heard that the law only applies to such systems. So they are ready for the response I have just given. Morris even calls it "an exceedingly naive argument". There are two popular Creationist rejoinders. The first is to pooh-pooh the concept of a closed system. The second is to change the subject.

There is something curious about the first rejoinder.

Here are two passages from Morris:

> Although it is true that the two laws of thermodynamics are defined in terms of isolated systems, it is also true that in the real world there is no such thing as an isolated system. *All* systems in reality are open systems and, furthermore, they are all open in greater or lesser degree, directly or indirectly, to the energy from the sun. Therefore, to say that the earth is a system open to the sun's energy does not explain anything, since the same statement is true for every other system as well!

> Obviously growth cannot occur in a closed system; the Second Law is in fact *defined* in terms of a closed system. However, this criterion is really redundant, because in the real world closed systems do not even exist! It is obvious that the Laws of Thermodynamics apply to open systems as well, since they have only been tested and proved on open systems!

For all the laurels heaped on classical thermodynamics, it appears that physicists have been somewhat misguided. They have introduced an unnecessary restriction, so that the laws of thermodynamics are not applicable to any existing systems. How fortunate that the Creationists are able to set them straight.

The concept of a thermodynamically closed system, like that of a frictionless plane or a perfectly rigid body, is an *idealization*. Let us recall our imaginary example of a closed system. I envisaged a perfectly insulated box within which bodies exchanged energy. Reality contains no such boxes. What we find are approximations to perfect insulation. To put the point more exactly, we find systems that can be treated *as if they were closed* because their energy exchange with the external environment is negligible in comparison with the energy flow within them. The laws of thermodynamics can be tested and confirmed (*not* proved) by investigating such systems, just as the laws of rigid-body mechanics can be tested and confirmed by investigating the behavior of things (like objects made of wood or metal) that are approximately rigid. What we cannot do is apply the laws of thermodynamics to systems for which the energy flow across the boundaries is significant in comparison with the energetic transactions within them. That would be like trying to use rigid-body mechanics to explain the motion of blobs of jelly. Because the systems studied in evolutionary theory exchange vast quantities of energy with the environment, they cannot be treated as if they were closed.

The Evolving Junkyard

The Creationist response, "Closed. Open. It's all the same," displays a hopeless misunderstanding of the second law of thermodynamics, born of ignorance of the role of idealization in physics. The second rejoinder appears to be more sophisticated. Morris advances what I shall call the "evolving junkyard" argument:

> It should be self-evident that the mere existence of an open system of some kind, with access to the sun's energy, does not of itself generate growth. The sun's energy may bathe the site of an automobile junk yard for a million years, but it will never cause the rusted, broken parts to grow together again into a functioning automobile. A beaker containing a fluid mixture of hydrochloric acid, water, salt, or any other combination of chemicals, may lie exposed to the sun for endless years, but the chemicals will never combine into a living bacterium or any other self-replicating organism. More likely, it would destroy any organism which might accidentally have been caught in it. Availability of energy (by the First Law of Thermodynamics) has in itself no mechanism for thwarting the basic decay principle enunciated by the Second Law of Thermodynamics. *Quantity* of energy is not the question, but *quality*!

As the history of science teaches us, great new ideas are seldom the property of a single individual. Wysong achieves the same insight: "If the decreased entropy and high orderliness of life is accounted for solely on the basis of open system thermodynamics, you might ask why other open systems don't likewise experience such ordering? [sic] In other words, why don't battered Volkswagons [sic] in junkyards order themselves into shiny new Cadillacs? A junkyard is an open system".

These passages might deceive us into thinking that a clever objection has been launched. But the issue has been shifted. Evolutionary theory was originally challenged to reconcile its claims of increasing organization and complexity with the second law of thermodynamics. The challenge is met by pointing out that there is no contradiction because the systems that are supposed to generate the trouble cannot be treated as good approximations to the ideal of a closed system. Creationists now ask why some open subsystems show decreasing entropy and others (cars in junkyards) do not. That is an entirely different question, and one that has an obvious answer. The simple answer is that the open systems that do not evolve have a different physiocochemical makeup from those that do evolve. Steel is significantly different from DNA. A detailed answer would explain exactly how both living things and automobiles change, in different ways, in accord with the laws of physics and chemistry. Even though the two systems are relevantly similar from a thermodynamical point of view, their physicochemical make-ups are relevantly different. Contrary to Wysong's suggestion, evolutionary biologists do not suppose that open-system thermodynamics *accounts for* the decreased entropy of life. Nobody alleged that having an open system *is sufficient* for decreased entropy. The point was to rebut a charge based on ignoring the restriction of the second law to closed systems. Evolutionary theory contends that decreased entropy is *possible* in an open system, not that it *must* happen in *any* open system.

To see how bad this argument really is, let me construct

an analogous line of reasoning. J. Fred Hailey, the attorney for the defense, offers an apparently conclusive case for his client's innocence. The victim could not have been done in by the defendant because the fire in the grate had consumed all the oxygen, so that the unfortunate party was dead prior to the defendant's arrival. Alas, the prosecutor has an eye for details and points out that a window was open, so that plenty of oxygen would have been available to keep the victim alive. But the defense never rests. Hailey retorts: "Window, no window, what's the difference? Besides, if the oxygen could keep the victim alive, why couldn't it revive the sofa on which he was sitting? Answer that, if you can!" The prosecutor is left (virtually) speechless.

Lurking behind the Creationist argument we find, once again, the randomness ploy. Morris and Wysong both use the "evolving junkyard" objection to conclude that some mechanism must be present in those open systems where entropy does decrease. They regard this conclusion as evidence that a designing hand guides the course of life. But this is a gigantic *nonsequitur.* Evolutionary theory never assumes that there is no explanation for the flow of energy in systems of living things. On the contrary, it supposes that physicochemical changes occur, and that energy is exchanged, in accordance with precise physical and chemical laws. Nonetheless, Creationists encumber the theory with the assumption that random processes are supposed to give rise to order and complexity. Wysong writes, "All observations confirm the inability of randomness to transform itself (open or closed system, it makes no difference) into high order." Such remarks thrive on confusing apparent randomness with irreducible randomness, and irreducible randomness with sheer chaos. According to evolutionary theory, the physicochemical constitution of certain open systems, together with the physicochemical features of their environment, causes those systems to maintain or decrease their entropy. Other open systems, with different constitutions or different environments are not so lucky. Classical thermodynamics does not preclude the possibility of either type of system because classical thermodynamics concerns itself with closed systems.

I would not have dealt with this objection at such length if the appeal to thermodynamics were not so popular a device among Creationists. (It is a mainstay of Creationist literature, and was duly discussed at the Arkansas trial.) However, my discussion does expose an interesting set of Creationist tactics. The original suggestion of contradiction between evolutionary theory and thermodynamics thrives on misstating the second law. Next, the Creationists consider responses that do not correct the formulation. This enables them to portray evolutionists as invoking the concept of a closed system out of desperation. They continue by distorting the role of idealization in science, and by changing the question. Instead of explaining how the evolution of systems of living things is consistent with the second law, scientists are supposed to *use* the second law to explain the precise details of energy exchange. Enter the randomness ploy, and the net result is confusion.

Evolution Is Testable and Scientific

Michael Ruse

Since much of the debate between Darwinists and creationists hinges on whether either can claim to be "scientific," it is naturally important to understand precisely what makes a theory scientific. Everyone agrees, of course, that scientific theories are somehow tested by experience, whether by personal observations or by carefully controlled laboratory studies. However, no single experience or group of experiences is enough to prove a general theory *true*. For this reason, the philosopher Karl Popper proposed that scientific theories are never proved true by experience, but only proved false. One consequence of Popper's view is a widely accepted criterion for what it means for a theory to be "scientific." According to Popper, a scientific theory must be "falsifiable" — that is, capable of being proven false (without *actually* being proven false). Curiously neither creationism nor the theory of natural selection seem to pass Popper's test.

Michael Ruse, *Darwinism Defended: A Guide to the Evolution Controversies*. Menlo Park, CA: The Benjamin/Cummings Publishing Company, 1982. Copyright © 1982 by The Benjamin/Cummings Publishing Company. Reproduced by permission of the author.

In this selection, Michael Ruse argues that Popper's test is an oversimplification. Even such clearly scientific theories as Sir Isaac Newton's theory of gravitation fail this test. Yet Newton's theory does make predictions that are tested in experience. Darwin's theory of natural selection also makes predictions that are tested in experience. It is not an empty tautology, as creationists claim, but genuine science.

Ruse is a professor of history and philosophy at the University of Guelph. His chief area of study is the philosophy of the biological sciences. His books include *The Philosophy of Biology* and *Sociobiology: Sense or Nonsense?*

The objection is as straightforward as it is popular and devastating, if well taken. It is claimed that Darwinian evolutionary theory—the critics usually lump together indifferently both past and present versions—is no genuine scientific theory at all. Despite appearances, it is just not about the empirical world; it is rather, at most, a speculative philosophy of nature, on a par with Plato's theory of forms or Swedenborgian theology [named after eighteenth-century theologian Emanuel Swedenborg]. It is, in short, a metaphysical wolf masquerading as a scientific lamb. And, although the critics hasten to assure us that there is nothing wrong with metaphysics, it is usually not too long before words like "slight" or "inadequate" or even "dismal" start to slip into the talk. All in all, we are left with the impression that Darwinism says nothing, and even if it did say something, it would not be *that* worth listening to. "Evolution is not a fact but a theory" is a charitable epitaph.

Just how does this objection come about? Let us see by starting with some general thoughts about the nature of science. I am sure that all will agree that there is a distinction to be drawn between those bodies of information or ideas that we want to label "scientific" and those that we do not, even though it is not always clear precisely where the distinction should be drawn. We want to distinguish for instance between something like the wave theory of light (albeit that today we may want to modify it in respects) and other sorts of claims, like those of literary criticism, philosophy, or religion. It may well make sense to say that "God is love"; one may well believe it with all one's heart. But, important though it is, somehow it does not seem to be a claim of quite the same type as (say) Snell's law [of refraction, named after Dutch mathematician Willebrord Snell], sin i / sin r = μ, or the claim that light goes in waves not particles.

It seems fairly clear that what distinguishes science from nonscience is the fact that scientific claims reflect, and somehow can be checked against, empirical experience—ultimately, the data that we get through our senses. The wave theory of light is about this physical world of ours; in some very important sense, God is not part of this world. We see light; we do not see God. But, how exactly does science reflect its empirical base? One might think that it is all simply a question of finding positive empirical evidence for scientific claims—evidence that is unobtainable for other sorts of claims. However, matters are a little more complex than this, because science does not deal with particulars, at least not directly and exclusively, but with generalities and universals. One's interest is not in this planet or that planet as such. Rather, one asks what each and every planet does, just as one asks what each and every light ray does.

But, this being so, simple checking and confirmation obviously cannot be enough. Suppose one has a general statement like Snell's law of refraction, and suppose also one has tested all kinds of light and all kinds of refracting media and found that the law holds. One can never preclude the possibility of a kind of light, or a type of medium, that violates the law. It is all a matter of simple logic; one just cannot definitively establish a universal statement by appealing to individual instances, however common or however positive they may be. Thousands of positive cases do not rule out one possible countercase.

Given this fact, many thinkers have therefore tried the opposite tack. Perhaps what distinguishes science is not that one can ever show it true, but that one can always knock it down! As [Evolutionist] T.H. Huxley was wont to say, the scientist must be prepared always to sit down before the facts, as a little child, ever prepared to give up the most cherished of theories should the empirical data dictate otherwise. Teasingly, Huxley used to say of his friend [philosopher] Herbert Spencer that his idea of a tragedy was that of a beautiful theory murdered by an ugly fact. Perhaps the edge to this quip reflects Huxley's belief that Spencer would go to any lengths to prevent murder being done—even to the extent of taking his theories out of science altogether.

Recently, the thinker who has stood most firmly and proudly in Huxley's tradition has been the philosopher [of science] Karl Popper. Starting from the logical point that, although many positive instances cannot confirm a universal statement, one negative instance can refute it, Popper argues that the essential mark of science—the "criterion of demarcation"—is that it is *falsifiable*.

> I shall not require of a scientific system that it shall be capable of being singled out, once and for all, in a positive sense; but I shall require that its logical form shall be such that it can be singled out, by means of empirical tests, in a negative sense: *it must be possible for an empirical scientific system to be refuted by experience* (Popper's italics).

Now, armed with this criterion, apparently we can distinguish a paradigmatic statement of science, like [seventeenth-century astronomer Johannes] Kepler's law that planets go in ellipses, from a statement of nonscience, "God is love." The former could be shown false by empirical observation and would indeed be shown false if one were, for example, to find a planet going in squares. The latter simply cannot be shown false by empirical data; it just is not falsifiable. In the face of the most horrific counterexamples—Vietnamese children screaming in agony from napalm burns—the believer continues to maintain that God is love. All is explained away as a function of freewill or some such thing.

Turning to science, or, more precisely, to claims that are made in the name of science, Popper and his sympathizers make short shrift of many areas of the social sciences. Freudian psychoanalytic theory is dismissed as incontrovertibly and irreparably unfalsifiable. But then moving on to biology, coming up against Darwinism, they feel compelled to make the same judgment: Darwinian evolutionary theory is unfalsifiable. Hence, the critical evaluation given at the beginning of this section: "I have come to the conclusion that Darwinism is not a testable scientific theory but a *metaphysical research programme*—a possible framework for testable scientific theories" (Popper's italics).

Since making this claim, Popper himself has modified his position somewhat; but, disclaimers aside, I suspect that even now he does not really believe that Darwinism in its modern form is genuinely falsifiable. If one relies heavily on natural selection and sexual selection, simultaneously downplaying drift, which of course is what the neo-Darwinian does do, then Popper feels that one has a nonfalsifiable theory. And, certainly, many followers agree that there is something conceptually flawed with Darwinism.

Just how precisely do the various critics make their case? Simply, it is argued that there is no way, either in practice or in principle, to put Darwinism (for ease, let us concentrate here on neo-Darwinism) to the test. For a start, testing requires prediction. One predicts something on the basis of a theory, checks to see if the prediction turns out true or false, and then rejects or retains one's theory on the basis of the results. But how can one make genuine predictions with Darwinism? Who could possibly predict what will happen to the elephant's trunk twenty-five million years down the road? Certainly not the Darwinian! And even if he could, there would be no one around to check out the prediction. Analogously, no one could step back to the Mesozoic to see the evolution of mammals and check if indeed natural selection was at work, nor could anyone spend a week or two (or century or two) in the Cretaceous to see if the dinosaurs, then going extinct, failed in the struggle for existence.

More importantly, argues the critic, even if one had a machine to go forward or back in time, it would make little difference! An essential claim of Darwinism devolves on the ubiquity of organic adaptation. The presumption is that physical characteristics have an adaptive value; they were preserved and selected because of their useful natures in the struggle for existence. But, in fact, it is easy to see that even in principle Darwinians guard themselves against counterarguments. . . .

There must be something dreadfully wrong with Darwinism. How can it be that something, which seems at first sight to be so all-encompassing and so impressively empirical, fails so dreadfully when subjected to searching inquiry? The critics think they know the source of all the trouble. Darwinism is no genuine scientific theory because it rests on a bogus mechanism: natural selection. Far from being an empirically testable, putative cause of evolutionary change, *natural selection is no scientific claim at all: it is a vacuous tautology.* Consider that natural selection states simply that a certain proportion of organisms, by definition the "fitter," survive and reproduce, whereas others do not. But, which are the "fitter"? Simply they are those that survive and reproduce! In other words, natural selection collapses into the analytically true statement that those that survive and reproduce are those that survive and reproduce. No wonder all the subareas of evolutionary thought come apart on close inspection. They put their trust in an empty statement. Indeed, one might feel that Popper is charitable in describing Darwinism as "metaphysical." Like Freudianism, it tells us nothing about the real world and fraudulently pretends that it does! . . .

Darwinism as Genuine Science

I believe this whole line of objection to be mistaken, absolutely and entirely. Given the survey of hard empirical inquiry we have seen thus far, the suggestion that Darwinism is nonempirical strikes me as bordering on the ludicrous. Protestations notwithstanding, the critics' arguments look suspiciously like some of those of Darwin's religious opponents. Popper, in fact, has been quite open about his inability to see how blind variation could lead to integrated, adaptive functioning in such a case as the eye or hand. Of this I am sure: there is an inability to grasp the implications of the balance hypothesis, with its claims about the ready supply of variation, available whenever selective pressures demand it. But, enough of what the critics can or cannot grasp. Onward, to the task of rebuttal! And, taking our cue from the critics, first let us make a few brief remarks of our own about science, before moving to direct defense of Darwinism.

The first point I want to make is that, although the major mark of science is undoubtedly the way in which it brushes against experience, and although undoubtedly falsifiability is important here, one must be careful not to take too literal or too narrow a reading of one's criteria. Other-

wise one will end up by counting out just a
didate for good science, including some that c
wants to include!

Put matters this way. There can be no doubt t
tonian gravitational theory qualifies as genuine, god ci-
ence. That it is perhaps now superceded does not touch this
point. But, right through its career, in respects, it was unfalsifiable! There were always parts of the theory that did not
work, in the sense that they led to predictions that went
against the evidence. The perihelion of Mercury, for instance, was a glaring anomaly for centuries. But Newtonians
did not reject their theory. They refused to let it be falsified,
hoping that some day a solution within the Newtonian
framework would be found—as almost invariably it was.
And the same element of unfalsifiability emerges when we
look at other claims, where the Newtonians speculated, but
simply had no way of checking whether their speculations
were true or false. Ad hoc hypotheses would be invented, or
counterevidence denied or shelved, until things fell neatly
into (Newtonian) place!

I do not want to exaggerate. The story of Newtonian theory in this century proves that ultimately the facts do prevail.
My point is that the mark of science is not to be decided by
pulling one or two claims from a theory and checking on
whether scientists would let them be falsified, or whether
they have even the first idea about checking them. In the
Newtonian case, one had a paradigmatic instance of a theory which integrates from many different areas—which exhibits a consilience of inductions—and which therefore was
judged as a whole. Newtonians could see many virtues in
their overall theory, particularly in its integrating simplicity.
They knew their theory was checkable in many parts—had
planets gone in squares, everyone would have looked
askance at the universal square law. However, Newtonians

knew that their theory came through check after check with flying colors. Prediction after prediction was confirmed. Hence, Newtonians tolerated a certain amount of counterevidence, thinking up ad hoc face-saving hypotheses and the like, and they lived with a number of uncheckable claims. Indeed, one might almost say that one expects a really good, powerful theory to exceed its grasp, and to get a little out of focus at the edges! Unfalsifiability here is not a sign of nonscience. It is a sign of sensible tolerance.

Now, all I have just said obviously applies with a vengeance to Darwinian evolutionary theory. Given its consilient nature, one must judge as a whole, not on the basis of isolated claims. Most particularly, it is just not fair to pick out one or two isolated areas, and then to make final, definitive judgments on the basis of them. One must look at the total picture and see if the theory is protected, in fact or in principle, from any empirical phenomenon that might impinge and refute it. If this is so, then obviously the theory must go—it is not real science. But if real checks are available, then tolerance is justifiable and justified elsewhere. If claims seem to go a little against the evidence, or (perhaps more importantly) Darwinians seem determined to fit the facts into their own pattern, then before condemning one must judge the whole. . . .

Is Natural Selection a Tautology?

We come now to the strongest and most crucial objection of all, namely that natural selection is a tautology, and that consequently the whole Darwinian edifice collapses into a truism. I believe that this objection is as wide of the mark as it is possible for an objection to be. In at least three respects, there is an empirical, nontautological, falsifiable basis to the mechanism cherished by Darwinians. That is to say, inasmuch as Darwinians want to apply models containing their mechanism to the living world, they commit themselves to at least three testable claims.

First, there is the claim that in the organic world there is a struggle for reproduction. Not all organisms that are born can and do survive and reproduce. Many fall by the wayside. This claim is undoubtedly true, but it is not a tautology. If everyone were identical, lived exactly the same length of time, and asexually produced one and only one offspring at the same point, there would be no struggle, no selection, and no evolution. Darwinism would be false; that is, any attempt to apply Darwinian models to the world would be fallacious.

Second, there is the central claim of Darwinians that they can apply their theory throughout the organic world, because success in the struggle is, on average, not random, but a function of the distinctive characteristics possessed by organisms. This is why we get adaptations. Again this is an empirical claim and could be false. Indeed, fairly obviously, supporters of the notion of genetic drift think that at times the claim is false. Drift is a highly contentious notion, but not even its strongest detractors think it a contradictory notion—which it would be were selection a tautology. It is logically impossible to apply to the world a model containing a contradiction. If drift is contradictory, why then was it necessary for [biologists Arthur J.] Cain and [Philip M.] Sheppard to spend as much time as they did out in the countryside looking at snails and thrushes?

Third, there is the claim that selection is systematic— what selection favors in one situation will be what selection favors in identical situations. In other words, one can apply a model with certain specified parameters again and again. A characteristic that helps an organism at one time and place can be expected to offer similar help in the same circumstances at different times and places. Thus, upon finding an arctic mammal with a white coat, an evolutionist confidently puts it down to an adaptive response to the snowy terrain, because this has been found to be the case for other arctic organisms. In a sense, this claim about the systematic nature of selection is the inductive element built into selection and is no doubt the reason why so many people think selection tautological. (When one has a common fallacy, it is important to show not merely why it is fallacious, but also why it is common.) It may be "obvious" that same causes in the same circumstances lead to same effects, but as the great Scottish philosopher David Hume (1740) showed us, it is not a logical necessity. . . .

On three points, therefore, natural selection transcends the tautological; that is to say, claims that the theory containing natural selection applies to the world require empirical, testable assertions. Additionally, within the core of modern evolutionary theory we have many other claims, and application of these latter is certainly not tautological. . . . The charge of unfalsifiability merits no more attention. Neither the central mechanism, nor Darwinian theory taken as a whole stand outside of the bounds of genuine empirical science. To go on arguing otherwise is to put ideology and ignorance above reason and experience.

Life Could Have Started Randomly

Richard Dawkins

While Darwin's theory addresses the process by which living organisms progressed from simple to complex forms, it does not explain how life began. Nevertheless, Darwin's theory does offer the promise that an explanation for the origin of life could be found without appealing to an act of creation. Given that complex life can evolve from simple life, it is only necessary to explain how the very simplest forms of life might have begun by sheer accident.

Richard Dawkins is one of the best known researchers and popular writers on evolutionary theory. His book *The Selfish Gene* is the classic study of altruistic behavior from a Darwinian perspective. That book is also credited with creating a whole new field of studies known as "memetics," which studies the spread of ideas (memorable units of information, called "memes") using Darwinian principles. Dawkins's other books include *Climbing Mount Improbable* and *Unweaving the Rainbow*.

In this selection Dawkins gives a brief lesson in understanding large-number probabilities. He then sketches out an intriguing (but not yet widely accepted) theory of the origin of life, the Cairns-Smith hypothesis. He argues that, with this theory, the origin of life is *so* probable that, rather than being mystified how life began, we should be mystified why we have not encountered evidence of life throughout the universe. Dawkins is *not* arguing that this theory is correct. He is, rather, arguing that it is easy to come up with a theory of the origin of life that satisfies the demands of probability, when these demands are correctly understood.

There are some would-be events that are too improbable to be contemplated, but we can't know this until we have done a calculation. And to do the calculation, we must know how much *time* was available, more generally how many *opportunities* were available, for the event to occur. Given infinite time, or infinite opportunities, anything is possible. The large numbers proverbially furnished by astronomy, and the large timespans characteristic of geology, combine to turn topsy-turvy our everyday estimates of what is expected and what is miraculous. I shall build up to this point using a specific example which is the other main theme of this chapter. This example is the problem of how life originated on Earth. To make the point clearly, I shall arbitrarily concentrate on one particular theory of the origin of life, although any one of the modern theories would have served the purpose.

We can accept a certain amount of luck in our explanations, but not too much. The question is, *how* much? The immensity of geological time entitles us to postulate more improbable coincidences than a court of law would allow but, even so, there are limits. Cumulative selection is the key to all our modern explanations of life. It strings a series of acceptably lucky events (random mutations) together in a nonrandom sequence so that, at the end of the sequence, the finished product carries the illusion of being very very lucky indeed, far too improbable to have come about by chance alone, even given a timespan millions of times longer than the age of the universe so far. Cumulative selection is the key but it had to get started, and we cannot escape the need to postulate a *single-step* chance event in the origin of cumulative selection itself. . . .

How Much Luck Is a Theory Allowed?

Now here is a fascinating thought. The answer to our question—of how much luck we are allowed to postulate—depends upon whether our planet is the only one that has life, or whether life abounds all around the universe. The one thing we know for certain is that life has arisen once, here on this very planet. But we have no idea at all whether there is life anywhere else in the universe. It is entirely possible that there isn't. Some people have calculated that there must be life elsewhere, on the following grounds (I won't point out the fallacy until afterwards). There are probably at least 10^{20} (i.e. 100 billion billion) roughly suitable planets in the universe. We know that life has arisen here, so it can't be *all* that improbable. Therefore it is almost inescapable that at least some among all those billions of billions of other planets has life.

The flaw in the argument lies in the inference that, *because life has arisen here,* it can't be too terribly improbable. You will notice that this inference contains the built-in assumption that whatever went on on Earth is likely to have gone on elsewhere in the universe, and this begs the whole question. In other words, that kind of statistical argument, that there must be life elsewhere in the universe because there is life here, builds in, as an assumption, what it is set-ting out to prove. This doesn't mean that the conclusion that life exists all around the universe is necessarily wrong. My guess is that it is probably right. It simply means that that particular argument that led up to it is no argument at all. It is just an assumption.

Let us, for the sake of discussion, entertain the alternative assumption that life has arisen only once, ever, and that was here on Earth. It is tempting to object to this assumption on the following emotional grounds. Isn't there something ter-ribly medieval about it? Doesn't it recall the time when the church taught that our Earth was the centre of the universe, and the stars just little pinpricks of light set in the sky for our delight (or, even more absurdly presumptuous, that the stars go out of their way to exert astrological influences on our little lives)? How very conceited to assume that, out of all the billions of billions of planets in the universe, our own little backwater of a world, in our own local backwater of a solar system, in our own local backwater of a galaxy, should have been singled out for life? Why, for goodness sake, should it have been *our* planet?

I am genuinely sorry, for I am heartily thankful that we have escaped from the small-mindedness of the medieval church and I despise modern astrologers, but I am afraid that the rhetoric about backwaters in the previous para-graph is just empty rhetoric. It is *entirely* possible that our backwater of a planet is literally the only one that has ever borne life. The point is that if there *were* only one planet that had ever borne life, then it would *have* to be our planet, for the very good reason that 'we' are here discussing the question! If the origin of life *is* such an improbable event that it happened on only one planet in the universe, then our planet has to be that planet. So, we can't use the fact that Earth has life to conclude that life must be probable enough to have arisen on another planet. Such an argument would be circular. We have to have some independent arguments about how easy or difficult it is for life to originate on a planet, before we can even begin to answer the question of how many other planets in the universe have life.

But that isn't the question we set out with. Our question was, how much luck are we allowed to assume in a theory of the origin of life on Earth? I said that the answer depends upon whether life has arisen only once, or many times. Begin by giving a name to the probability, however low it is, that life will originate on any randomly designated planet of some particular type. Call this number the spontaneous generation probability or SGP. It is the SGP that we shall arrive at if we sit down with our chemistry textbooks, or strike sparks through plausible mixtures of atmospheric gases in our laboratory, and calculate the odds of replicating molecules springing spontaneously into existence in a typical planetary atmosphere. Suppose that our best guess of the SGP is some very very small number, say one in a billion. This is obviously such a small probability that we haven't the faintest hope of duplicating such a fantastically lucky, miraculous event as the origin of life in our laboratory experiments. Yet if we assume, as we are perfectly entitled to do for the sake of argument, that life has originated only once in the universe, it follows that we are *allowed* to postulate a very large amount of luck in a theory, because there are so many planets in the universe where life *could* have originated. If, as one estimate has it, there are 100 billion billion planets, this is 100 billion times greater than even the very low SGP that we postulated. To conclude this argument, the maximum amount of luck that we are allowed to assume, before we reject a particular theory of the origin of life, has odds of one in N, where N is the number of suitable planets in the universe. There is a lot hidden in that word 'suitable', but let us put an upper limit of 1 in 100 billion billion for the maximum amount of luck that this argument entitles us to assume. . . .

The Cairns-Smith Hypothesis

Most textbooks give greatest weight to the family of theories based on an organic 'primeval soup'. It seems probable that the atmosphere of Earth before the coming of life was like that of other planets which are still lifeless. There was no oxygen, plenty of hydrogen and water, carbon dioxide, very likely some ammonia, methane and other simple organic gases. Chemists know that oxygen-free climates like this tend to foster the spontaneous synthesis of organic compounds. They have set up in flasks miniature reconstructions of conditions on the early Earth. They have passed through the flasks electric sparks simulating lightning, and ultraviolet light, which would have been much stronger before the Earth had an ozone layer shielding it from the sun's rays. The results of these experiments have been exciting. Organic molecules, some of them of the same general types as are normally only found in living things, have spontaneously assembled themselves in these flasks. Neither DNA nor RNA has appeared, but the building blocks of these large molecules, called purines and pyrimidines, have. So have the building blocks of proteins, amino acids. The missing link for this class of theories is still the origin of replication. The building blocks haven't come together to form a self-replicating chain like RNA. Maybe one day they will.

But, in any case, the organic primeval-soup theory is not the one I have chosen for my illustration of the kind of solution that we must look for. I did choose it in my first book, *The Selfish Gene*, so I thought that here I would fly a kite for a somewhat less-fashionable theory (although it recently has started gaining ground), which seems to me to have at least a sporting chance of being right. Its audacity is appealing, and it does illustrate well the properties that any satisfying theory of the origin of life must have. This is the 'inorganic mineral' theory of the Glasgow chemist Graham Cairns-Smith, first proposed 20 years ago and since developed and elaborated in three books, the latest of which, *Seven Clues to the Origin of Life*, treats the origin of life as a mystery needing a Sherlock Holmes solution.

Cairns-Smith's view of the DNA/protein machinery is that it probably came into existence relatively recently, perhaps as recently as three billion years ago. Before that there were many generations of cumulative selection, based upon some quite different replicating entities. Once DNA was there, it proved to be so much more efficient as a replicator, and so much more powerful in its effects on its own replication, that the original replication system that spawned it was cast off and forgotten. The modern DNA machinery, according to this view, is a late-comer, a recent usurper of the role of fundamental replicator, having taken over that role from an earlier and cruder replicator. There may even have been a whole series of such usurpations, but the original replication process must have been sufficiently simple to have come about through what I have dubbed 'single-step selection'.

Chemists divide their subject into two main branches, organic and inorganic. Organic chemistry is the chemistry of one particular element, carbon. Inorganic chemistry is all the rest. Carbon is important and deserves to have its own private branch of chemistry, partly because life chemistry is all carbon-chemistry, and partly because those same properties that make carbon-chemistry suitable for life also make it suitable for industrial processes, such as those of the plastics industry. The essential property of carbon atoms that makes them so suitable for life and for industrial synthetics, is that they join together to form a limitless repertoire of different kinds of very large molecules. Another element that has some of these same properties is silicon. Although the chemistry of modern Earth-bound life is all carbon-chemistry, this may not be true all over the universe, and it may not always have been true on this Earth. Cairns-Smith believes that the original life on this planet was based on self-replicating inorganic crystals such as silicates. If this is true, organic replicators, and eventually DNA, must later have taken over or usurped the role.

He gives some arguments for the general plausibility of this idea of 'takeover'. An arch of stones, for instance, is a stable structure capable of standing for many years even if there is no cement to bind it. Building a complex structure by evolution is like trying to build a mortarless arch if you are allowed to touch only one stone at a time. Think about the task naïvely, and it can't be done. The arch will stand once the last stone is in place, but the intermediate stages are unstable. It's quite easy to build the arch, however, if you are allowed to subtract stones as well as add them. Start by building a solid heap of stones, then build the arch resting on top of this solid foundation. Then, when the arch is all in position, including the vital keystone at the top, carefully remove the supporting stones and, with a modicum of luck, the arch will remain standing. Stonehenge is incomprehensible until we realize that the builders used some kind of scaffolding, or perhaps ramps of earth, *which are no longer there*. We can see only the end-product, and have to infer the vanished scaffolding. Similarly, DNA and protein are two pillars of a stable and elegant arch, which persists once all its parts simultaneously exist. It is hard to imagine it arising by any step-by-step process unless some earlier scaffolding has completely disappeared. That scaffolding must itself have been built by an earlier form of cumulative selection, at whose nature we can only guess. But it must have been based upon replicating entities with power over their own future.

Cairns-Smith's guess is that the original replicators were crystals of inorganic materials, such as those found in clays and muds. A crystal is just a large orderly array of atoms or molecules in the solid state. Because of properties that we can think of as their 'shape', atoms and small molecules tend naturally to pack themselves together in a fixed and orderly manner. It is almost as though they 'want' to slot together in a particular way, but this illusion is just an inadvertent consequence of their properties. Their 'preferred' way of slotting together shapes the whole crystal. It also means that, even in a large crystal such as a diamond, any part of the crystal is *exactly* the same as any other part, except where there are flaws. If we could shrink ourselves to the atomic scale, we would see almost endless rows of atoms, stretching to the horizon in straight lines—galleries of geometric repetition.

Since it is replication we are interested in, the first thing we must know is, can crystals replicate their structure? Crystals are made of myriads of layers of atoms (or equivalent), and each layer builds upon the layer below. Atoms (or ions; the difference needn't concern us) float around free in solution, but if they happen to encounter a crystal they have a natural tendency to slot into position on the surface of the crystal. A solution of common salt contains sodium ions and chloride ions jostling about in a more or less chaotic fashion. A crystal of common salt is a packed, orderly array of sodium ions alternating with chloride ions at right angles to one another. When ions floating in the water happen to bump into the hard surface of the crystal, they tend to stick. And they stick in just the right places to cause a new layer to be added to the crystal just like the layer below. So once a crystal gets started it grows, each layer being the same as the layer below.

Sometimes crystals spontaneously start to form in solution. At other times they have to be 'seeded', either by particles of dust or by small crystals dropped in from elsewhere. Cairns-Smith invites us to perform the following experiment. Dissolve a large quantity of photographer's 'hypo' fixer in very hot water. Then let the solution cool down, being careful not to let any dust drop in. The solution is now 'supersaturated', ready and waiting to make crystals, but with no seed crystals to start the process going. I quote from Cairns-Smith's *Seven Clues to the Origin of Life*:

> Carefully take the lid off the beaker, drop one tiny piece of 'hypo' crystal onto the surface of the solution, and watch amazed at what happens. Your crystal grows visibly: it breaks up from time to time and the pieces also grow . . . Soon your beaker is crowded with crystals, some several centimetres long. Then after a few minutes it all stops. The magic solution has lost its power—although if you want another performance just re-heat and re-cool the beaker . . . to be supersaturated means to have more dissolved than there ought to be . . . the cold supersaturated solution almost literally did not know what to do. It had to be 'told' by adding a piece of crystal that already had its units (billions and billions of them) packed together in the way that is characteristic for 'hypo' crystals. The solution had to be seeded.

Some chemical substances have the potential to crystallize in two alternative ways. Graphite and diamonds, for instance, are both crystals of pure carbon. Their atoms are identical. The two substances differ from each other only in the geometric pattern with which the carbon atoms are packed. In diamonds, the carbon atoms are packed in a tetrahedral pattern which is extremely stable. This is why diamonds are so hard. In graphite the carbon atoms are arranged in flat hexagons layered on top of each other. The bonding between layers is weak, and they therefore slide over each other, which is why graphite feels slippery and is used as a lubricant. Unfortunately you can't crystallize diamonds out of a solution by seeding them, as you can with hypo. If you could, you'd be rich; no on second thoughts you wouldn't, because any fool could do the same.

Self-Replication of Inorganic Crystals

Now suppose we have a supersaturated solution of some substance, like hypo in that it was eager to crystallize out of solution, and like carbon in that it was capable of crystallizing in either of two ways. One way might be somewhat like graphite, with the atoms arranged in layers, leading to little flat crystals; while the other way gives chunky, diamond-shaped crystals. Now we simultaneously drop into our supersaturated solution a tiny flat crystal and a tiny chunky crystal. We can describe what would happen in an elaboration of Cairns-Smith's description of his hypo experiment. You watch amazed at what happens. Your two crystals grow visibly: they break up from time to time and the pieces also grow. Flat crystals give rise to a population of flat crystals. Chunky crystals give rise to a population of chunky crystals. If there is any tendency for one type of crystal to grow and split more quickly than the other, we shall have a simple kind of natural selection. But the process still lacks a vital ingredient in order to give rise to evolutionary change. That ingredient is hereditary variation, or something equivalent to it. Instead of just two types of crystal, there must be a whole range of minor variants that form lineages of like shape, and that sometimes 'mutate' to produce new shapes. Do real crystals have something corresponding to hereditary mutation?

Clays and muds and rocks are made of tiny crystals. They are abundant on Earth and probably always have been. When you look at the surface of some types of clay and other minerals with a scanning electron microscope you see an amazing and beautiful sight. Crystals grow like rows of flowers or cactuses, gardens of inorganic rose petals, tiny spirals like cross-sections of succulent plants, bristling organ pipes, complicated angular shapes folded as if in miniature crystalline origami, writhing growths like worm casts or squeezed toothpaste. The ordered patterns become even more striking at greater levels of magnification. At levels that betray the actual position of atoms, the surface of a crystal is seen to have all the regularity of a machine-woven piece of herringbone tweed. But—and here is the vital point— there are flaws. Right in the middle of an expanse of orderly herringbone there can be a patch, identical to the rest except that it is twisted round at a different angle so that the 'weave' goes off in another direction. Or the weave may lie in the same direction, but each row has 'slipped' half a row to one side. Nearly all naturally occurring crystals have flaws. And once a flaw has appeared, it tends to be copied as subsequent layers of crystal encrust themselves on top of it. . . .

To speculate a little further, suppose that a variant of a clay improves its own chances of being deposited, by damming up streams. This is an inadvertent consequence of the peculiar defect structure of the clay. In any stream in which this kind of clay exists, large, stagnant shallow pools form above dams, and the main flow of water is diverted into a new course. In these still pools, more of the same kind of clay is laid down. A succession of such shallow pools proliferates along the length of any stream that happens to be 'infected' by seeding crystals of this kind of clay. Now, because the main flow of the stream is diverted, during the dry season the shallow pools tend to dry up. The clay dries and cracks in the sun, and the top layers are blown off as dust. Each dust particle inherits the characteristic defect structure of the parent clay that did the damming, the structure that gave it its damming properties. By analogy with the genetic information raining down on the canal from my willow tree, we could say that the dust carries 'instructions' for how to dam streams and eventually make more dust. The dust spreads far and wide in the wind, and there is a good chance that some particles of it will happen to land in another stream, hitherto not 'infected' with the seeds of this kind of dam-making clay. Once infected by the right sort of dust, a new stream starts to grow crystals of dam-making clay, and the whole depositing, damming, drying, eroding cycle begins again. . . .

Now to move on to the next stage of the argument. Some lineages of crystals might happen to catalyse the synthesis of new substances that assist in their passage down the 'generations'. These secondary substances would not (not at first, anyway) have had their own lineages of ancestry and descent, but would have been manufactured anew by each generation of primary replicators. They could be seen as tools of the replicating crystal lineages, the beginnings of primitive 'phenotypes'. Cairns-Smith believes that *organic* molecules were prominent among non-replicating 'tools' of his inorganic crystalline replicators. Organic molecules frequently are used in the commercial inorganic chemical industry because of their effects on the flow of fluids, and on the break-up or growth of inorganic particles: just the sorts of effects, in short, that could have influenced the 'success' of lineages of replicating crystals. For instance, a clay mineral with the lovely name montmorillonite tends to break up in the presence of small amounts of an organic molecule with the less-lovely name carboxymethyl cellulose. Smaller quantities of carboxymethyl cellulose, on the other hand, have just the opposite effect, helping to stick montmorillonite particles together. Tannins, another kind of organic molecule, are used in the oil industry to make muds easier to drill. If oil-drillers can exploit organic molecules to manipulate the flow and drillability of mud, there is no reason why cumulative selection should not have led to the same kind of exploitation by self-replicating minerals.

At this point Cairns-Smith's theory gets a sort of free bonus of added plausibility. It so happens that other chemists, supporting more conventional organic 'primeval soup' theories, have long accepted that clay minerals would have been a help. To quote one of them (D. M. Anderson), 'It is widely accepted that some, perhaps many, of the abiotic chemical reactions and processes leading to the origin on Earth of replicating micro-organisms occurred very early in the history of Earth in close proximity to the surfaces of clay minerals and other inorganic substrates.' This writer goes on to list five 'functions' of clay minerals in assisting the origin of organic life, for instance 'Concentration of chemical reactants by adsorption'. We needn't spell the five out here, or even understand them. From our point of view, what matters is that each of these five 'functions' of clay minerals can be twisted round the other way. It shows the close association that can exist between organic chemical synthesis and clay surfaces. It is therefore a bonus for the theory that clay replicators synthesized organic molecules and used them for their own purposes. . . .

Can a Theory Be *Too* Plausible?

It is often pointed out that chemists have failed in their attempts to duplicate the spontaneous origin of life in the laboratory. This fact is used as if it constituted evidence against the theories that those chemists are trying to test. But actually one can argue that we should be worried if it turned out to be very easy for chemists to obtain life spontaneously in the test-tube. This is because chemists' experiments last for years not thousands of millions of years, and because only a handful of chemists, not thousands of millions of chemists, are engaged in doing these experiments.

If the spontaneous origin of life turned out to be a probable enough event to have occurred during the few man-decades in which chemists have done their experiments, then life should have arisen many times on Earth, and many times on planets within radio range of Earth. . . .

So we have arrived at the following paradox. If a theory of the origin of life is sufficiently 'plausible' to satisfy our subjective judgement of plausibility, it is then *too* 'plausible' to account for the paucity of life in the universe as we observe it. According to this argument, the theory we are looking for has *got* to be the kind of theory that seems implausible to our limited, Earth-bound, decade-bound imaginations. Seen in this light, both Cairns-Smith's theory and the primeval-soup theory seem if anything in danger of erring on the side of being too plausible! Having said all this I must confess that, because there is so much uncertainty in the calculations, if a chemist *did* succeed in creating spontaneous life I would not actually be disconcerted!

Darwinism Is Not Immoral

James Rachels

Presumably science is concerned with facts, not with values. Yet some scientific theories do seem to imply moral consequences. When the theory of natural selection was first proposed, some philosophers, notably Herbert Spencer, tried to translate the principles of evolution directly into human moral values. Modern philosophers consider this to be a transparent error, and even give the error its own name: the naturalistic fallacy.

James Rachels is a professor of philosophy at the University of Alabama–Birmingham. His chief area of interest is ethics, including biomedical ethics. His other writings include *The Elements of Moral Philosophy* and a classic essay on euthanasia, "Active and Passive Euthanasia."

In this selection Rachels explains Herbert Spencer's original argument for a Darwinian morality, pointing out that it is actually a more sophisticated argument (and more humane) than the view usually attributed to him. Rachels then explains G.E. Moore's refutation of the argument. Rachels

James Rachels, *Created from Animals: The Moral Implications of Darwinism.* New York: Oxford University Press, 1990. Copyright © 1990 by James Rachels. Reproduced by permission.

concludes that Moore (and all modern philosophers) are right to reject the view that Darwinism can be transformed into a moral theory.

A few months after publication of the *Origin*, Darwin wrote to [geologist Charles] Lyell, with obvious amusement: 'I have noted in a Manchester newspaper a rather good squib, showing that I have proved "might is right" and therefore Napoleon is right and every cheating tradesman is also right.' The Manchester editorialist thought this was a reason for rejecting Darwinism—obviously, a theory with such implications should not be accepted. Others, however, would soon take a different view. They would accept Darwin's theory, and conclude that the morality of ruthlessness was a good lesson to be learned from it.

Herbert Spencer's Social Darwinism

Although it was not really fair to him, the name of Herbert Spencer was most commonly associated with this idea. Spencer, eleven years younger than Darwin, came from a free-thinking Derbyshire family and as a young man was attracted to radical causes such as the suffragist movement. He wandered from job to job, dabbled in journalism, and ended up as a kind of free-lance writer on intellectual subjects. In 1851 he published a book, *Social Statics*, advocating a version of evolutionary theory inspired by Lamarck and drawing lessons from it about the nature of happiness. As science, the work had little merit, which is not surprising considering that Spencer was largely self-educated and had not bothered to train himself in natural history. Although his theory received scant attention from serious naturalists, in the small world of British intellectuals Spencer became a 'somebody', and after the publication of *The Origin of Species*, his reputation grew.

But if Spencer was no scientist, he was a philosopher of some talent. As Darwin's influence spread, it became fashionable to think that evolutionary ideas could be adapted to explain a broad range of human phenomena, from art and religion to politics and ethics. Spencer was in the forefront of this movement. Although Darwin sometimes expressed dismay about Spencer's writings, especially the scientific portions, he generally held him in high regard. In 1870 Darwin wrote to a friend,

> It has also pleased me to see how thoroughly you appreciate (and I do not think that this is in general true with the men of science) H. Spencer; I suspect that hereafter he will be looked at as by far the greatest living philosopher in England; perhaps equal to any that have lived.

Darwin was a poor prophet. Today almost no one reads Spencer. Far from being regarded as a great philosopher, university courses in the history of the subject may not even mention him at all. Nonetheless, he was an ingenious man, and he produced a series of interesting books 'applying' the theory of evolution (as well as other scientific enthusiasms of the day) to the main problems of philosophy. In their day his books made quite a stir.

Spencer's popularity was greatest in America. As early as 1864, the *Atlantic Monthly* proclaimed that 'Mr Spencer represents the scientific spirit of the age.' The president of Columbia University went even farther: 'We have in Herbert Spencer', said F.A.P. Barnard, 'not only the profoundest thinker of our time, but the most capacious and most powerful intellect of all time.' Such was the American enthusiasm for the man who sought to draw lessons from Darwinism. What earned Spencer such extravagant praise? Partly it was a general exuberance for the new 'scientific' approach to understanding human affairs. But the enthusiasm was also due to the way in which Spencer's doctrines seemed to vindicate American capitalism. 'The survival of the fittest' was quickly interpreted as an ethical precept that sanctioned cutthroat economic competition.

Capitalist giants such as John D. Rockefeller and Andrew Carnegie regularly invoked what they took to be 'Darwinian' principles to explain the ethics of the American system. Rockefeller, in a talk to his Sunday School class, proclaimed that 'The growth of large business is merely a survival of the fittest . . . The American Beauty rose can be produced in the splendor and fragrance which bring cheer to its beholder only by sacrificing the early buds which grew up around it. This is not an evil tendency in business. It is merely the working-out of a law of nature and a law of God.' Carnegie, who became a close friend of Spencer's, was equally rhapsodic: in defending the concentration of wealth in the hands of a few big businessmen, he proclaimed that 'While the law may sometimes be hard for the individual, it is best for the race, because it ensures the survival of the fittest in every department.' Rockefeller's and Carnegie's understanding of natural selection was only a little better than that of the Manchester editorialist.

Some of Spencer's less cautious writings encouraged this interpretation. He was a robust champion of self-reliant individualism and an advocate of free-enterprise economics. Moreover, he was delighted to have the friendship of such men as Carnegie, who entertained him lavishly when he visited America. But he was not a crude thinker. In his works on ethical theory, Spencer took a sober and cautious approach. In those works, we do not find facile 'deductions' of economic individualism from evolutionary principles. Nor do we find the vulgar slogans that were associated with his name: he did not say that 'Whatever gives one an advantage in the struggle for life is right'; nor did he try to make 'the survival of the fittest' into some sort of ethical maxim. His view was more sophisticated than that, and his theoretical treatises were careful works that could be read, and sometimes admired, by serious philosophers.

Spencer's *Data of Ethics* appeared in 1879. In it he begins by announcing the 'pressing need' for 'the establishment of rules of conduct on a scientific basis', because the advent of Darwinism had destroyed the old verities. 'Now that moral injunctions are losing the authority given by their supposed sacred origin,' he says, 'the secularization of morals is becoming imperative.' Of course, Spencer thought he knew how to do this.

Ethics, Spencer said, could be defined as the area that 'has for its subject-matter that form which universal conduct assumes during the last stages of its evolution'. Our conduct, like everything else about us, has evolved; and Spencer assumed that as a result of this evolution humans have now achieved 'higher' forms of behaviour. Of course, this untroubled use of such notions as 'higher' and 'lower' was very unDarwinian. Darwin would never have spoken of 'the last stage' of evolution, as though it were a process that terminates in some sort of final perfection. Spencer seems not to have understood, or at least he did not accept, Darwin's point that adaptations are not 'directed' to any particular end. There is no 'more evolved' or 'less evolved' in Darwinian theory; there are only the different paths taken by different species, largely, but not entirely, in response to different environmental pressures. Natural selection is a process that, in principle, goes on forever, moving in no particular direction; it moves this way and that, eliminating some species and altering others, as environmental conditions change.

But Spencer began as a Lamarckian, and never shook off the Lamarckian notion that evolution is driven by an internal impulse towards 'higher forms'. So for him the crucial question was: Towards what end is evolution aimed? In what direction does it inevitably take us? His answer was that all creatures, including humans, have evolved patterns of behaviour that serve to increase the length and comfort of their lives. (He mentions, but does not emphasize, that evolution also favours conduct that increases the number of one's progeny.) The 'highest' form of conduct is, therefore, the conduct that is most effective in achieving these goals. What type of conduct is this? According to Spencer, the most effective conduct is the co-operative behaviour of people living together in 'permanently peaceful societies'.

Spencer is not clear about why social living is so important from an evolutionary point of view, but by emphasizing it he was able to account for one of the central features of morality, namely obligations to other people. Ethical conduct is, at least in part, unselfish conduct, and so any plausible account of ethics must explain the basis of other-regarding obligations. By conceiving of 'fully evolved conduct' as the conduct of people in *communities*, Spencer made a place for the duty of beneficence. At any rate, whatever his reason for introducing this notion, he says that 'the permanently peaceful community' represents 'the limit of evolution' as far as conduct is concerned, and so he concludes that it is 'the subject-matter of ethics'.

Having argued this to his satisfaction, Spencer then turns to the analysis of 'good and bad conduct'. He contends that 'good conduct' can be understood in the same way that we understand the notion of a 'good knife' or a 'good pair of boots'. (Socrates was also fond of this type of comparison.) Knives have a purpose; they are used for cutting. A good knife, therefore, is one that cuts easily and efficiently. Similarly, to discover the meaning of good conduct, we may ask what conduct is for, and then what type of conduct serves this purpose best. But this, it turns out, is a matter he has already settled: the purpose of conduct is to increase the length and quality of one's life and to secure offspring. This is the type of conduct that evolution produces. Therefore, Spencer concluded,

> The conduct to which we apply the name good, is the relatively more evolved conduct; and bad is the name we apply to conduct which is relatively less evolved . . . Moreover, just as we saw that evolution becomes the highest possible when the conduct simultaneously achieves the greatest totality of life in self, in offspring, and in fellow-men; so here we see that the conduct called good rises to the conduct conceived as best, when it fulfills all three classes at the same time.

In summary, then, Spencer's argument seems to have been this:

1. The behavioural characteristics of a species are among the characteristics that are shaped by the evolutionary process.
2. Evolution favours conduct that tends to lengthen individual lives, increase the quality of life, and, not coincidentally, secure offspring. 'More evolved' conduct is conduct that does this job better.
3. Moreover, the *purpose* of conduct is to achieve the goals of longer and better life and more offspring.
4. These goals are best achieved when people live together, cooperating with one another, in peaceful communities.
5. It follows that the 'highest' or 'most evolved' form of conduct is conduct that creates and enhances 'permanently peaceful communities'.
6. Therefore, good conduct may be defined as conduct that achieves these goals, while bad conduct is conduct that frustrates these goals. Or; as Spencer says, 'good conduct' is 'more evolved conduct'.

Here, then, we have an ambitious, if still somewhat sketchy, theory of ethics, explicitly based on evolutionary ideas. What was to be made of it? For a while, it seemed to be a viable theory, at least no worse than other contenders in the field, and having the considerable advantage of connecting ethics with the latest scientific theory about human nature. But Spencer's popularity was short-lived. For philosophers, the publication of G.E. Moore's *Principia Ethica* in 1903 sounded its death knell.

The Naturalistic Fallacy

Moore was a Cambridge philosopher at the beginning of what was to be a long and distinguished career. His first book would become a classic, not so much for its positive claims as for its style of argument, its redefinitions of philosophical questions, and its sharp criticisms of familiar views. One of Moore's chief contentions was that all naturalistic theories of morality commit a certain mistake, which he called 'the naturalistic fallacy'. Moore used Spencer's view to illustrate how theories fall into this error. Only a dozen pages were devoted to Spencer, but Moore's charges seemed, to many readers, unanswerable. His arguments were all the more persuasive because Moore's reading of Spencer was balanced and fair, and because Moore was himself an admirer of Darwin—he was no anti-scientific yahoo, out to buttress traditional morality. After Moore's demolition, Spencer's view would seem hopelessly naïve. But it was not merely Spencer's specific formulations that were found to be defective. If Moore was right, the natural sciences, including evolutionary biology, were simply irrelevant to ethics. Readers of *Principia Ethica* would come away with the conviction that Spencer had been right about at least one thing: the foundations of ethics needed to be rethought. But most would also be convinced that 'evolutionary ethics' was a fundamentally confused idea that should have no place in the rethinking.

Taking some liberties, Moore's central argument can be stated briefly. The 'naturalistic fallacy' is committed by any theory that seeks to define ethics in naturalistic terms. Ethics has to do with what is good or right—in other words, with what *ought to be* the case. Naturalistic theories identify goodness or rightness with 'natural' properties of things—in other words, with facts about what *is* the case. But that is always a mistake. The naturalistic fallacy, therefore, is the fallacy of confusing what ought to be the case with what is the case. Spencer's theory is an example. Spencer holds that 'good conduct' is the same as 'relatively more evolved conduct'. But when we think about it, we can see that 'good' and 'relatively more evolved' are quite different notions. Whether something is good is a matter of evaluation; whereas whether something is relatively more evolved is a matter of fact. The two are not the same, and so Spencer's theory fails. . . .

Moore was right to reject Spencer's view. Spencer's theory was not one that Darwinians could accept. Moore pointed out (what we have already observed) that Spencer's understanding of evolution was inconsistent with Darwinian notions. Darwin tried to avoid such terms as 'higher' and 'lower' when referring to stages of development—a distinctive feature of his theory was its denial that evolutionary change is associated with any purpose or 'direction'. There is no advancement and no regression; there is only change. Spencer's ethical theory, on the other hand, depended on a Lamarckian stance, on seeing some conduct as 'more evolved' than other conduct. In this way he sneaked in an evaluative element that is alien to Darwinian conceptions. As Darwin clearly recognized, we are not entitled—not on evolutionary grounds, at any rate—to regard our own adaptive behaviour as 'better' or 'higher' than that of the cockroach, who, after all, is adapted equally well to life in its own environmental niche. Natural selection favours creatures whose conduct enables them to win the competition to reproduce. Not only human behaviour, but the behaviour of countless other species, has this result. If Spencer had accepted this fundamental point, his theory would never have been conceived.

Moore's book was tremendously influential. Coming just after the turn of the century, it defined the problems that moral philosophers were to discuss for the next six decades. Evolutionary ethics was now removed from the philosophical agenda; and soon the independence of ethics from *all* the sciences would become an article of faith. By 1903, the year *Principia Ethica* was published, Spencer's books had sold a phenomenal 368,755 copies in America alone. But the vogue was over. It seems somehow fitting that, in that same year, Spencer died.

People tend to have strong opinions about whether evolution is fact or fiction. Most scientists accept evolution, and nonscientists who accept evolution are convinced that the overwhelming weight of scientific evidence is on their side. People who reject evolution often do so because they are convinced that evolution is inconsistent with their religious beliefs. They believe that the Bible provides us with a true account of the history of the earth and of the history of life on Earth. They believe that this account contradicts the account given by those scientists who assume that evolution takes place. However, people who reject evolution do not generally reject science itself, or the principles of scientific reasoning. If the Bible gives a true account of the history of the earth, then the evidence obtained by observing the world should ultimately support, not contradict, the account given in the Bible. Scientists sometimes make mistakes. Perhaps the scientists who accept evolution are misinterpreting the evidence. Both sides claim that the evidence so far collected supports their view.

Who is right about evolution? In order to form your own opinion, you need to think critically about the evidence that each side offers. Thinking critically does not mean finding negative things to say about an author or the arguments he or she presents. It means, first, trying to understand the argument and, second, evaluating whether that argument is persuasive for legitimate reasons. This epilogue describes a technique for understanding and evaluating scientific arguments, and it allows you to practice using this technique on the articles in this book.

The Author

When nonexperts try to form opinions on scientific questions, they often do so by considering the reputation and qualifications of the author whose article they are reading. Nowadays this is relatively easy to do, since information about almost any author can be found on the Internet. Using any popular search engine, it is not difficult to find out what degrees an author has earned, whether he or she holds an academic position, and whether he or she is the author of other works on the same or related topics. In this book, the editor has provided a small amount of information about each author that you can use to begin evaluating that author's standing in the scientific community. Since you probably have access to the Internet, you can (and should) supplement this information with research of your own.

However, as valuable as it may be to know something about an author, it is possible that some authors who advocate unpopular views have been prevented from acquiring more impressive credentials precisely because their views are unpopular. Any author has the right to be judged not just on his or her credentials but also on the soundness of his or her reasoning.

Hypothetical Reasoning

Scientists are not just interested in facts but also in explanations. That is, they are not just interested in what the world is like, but also in how it got that way. For example, if you walk into your room and find your homework (which you left stacked neatly on your desk) scattered all over the floor, you may be curious to know why it is there. Simply observing that your homework is on the floor is not yet to think like a scientist. You begin thinking like a scientist when you begin to ask what could have caused your homework to be on the floor. Perhaps your homework was blown off the desk by the wind. Perhaps your cat knocked it off. Perhaps your house has a poltergeist (a ghost that tends to throw things around). Which of these explanations is best? A proposed explanation is called a hypothesis, and the reasoning that is used to evaluate a hypothesis is called hypothetical reasoning. The goal of hypothetical reasoning is to decide which explanation or hypothesis is best. Using hypothetical reasoning does not guarantee that we will arrive at the correct explanation. It is simply in the nature of hypothetical reasoning that alternative explanations are always possible, and the explanation that appears to be best may not always be true. For example, to support the hypothesis that your homework was blown off your desk by the wind, you may observe that a window is open and that it has been windy all day. This certainly suggests that the wind hypothesis is the best explanation. Even so, it is still possible that your cat (or a poltergeist) was the real cause. Hypothetical reasoning never produces certainty. Scientists use hypothetical reasoning anyway, because no other form of reasoning involves the kind of speculation that allows us to discover new facts about the world.

To use hypothetical reasoning to analyze the articles in this book, use these five steps:

1. Identify a fact that the author wishes to explain and state the author's hypothesis to explain that fact.
2. Gather the author's evidence supporting that hypothesis.
3. Evaluate the way in which this evidence supports the hypothesis.
4. Consider alternative hypotheses, or explanations.
5. Draw a conclusion about the author's hypothesis.

Using hypothetical reasoning to examine several articles on evolution may give you a better appreciation for arguments on each side. It will probably not give you a final answer to the big question of whether evolution is fact or fiction. In the following sections, we will use hypothetical reasoning to examine some of the articles in this book critically. You can then practice applying hypothetical reasoning to other articles.

1. State the author's hypothesis.

A hypothesis is not a statement of someone's mere opinion, and it is not true merely because someone says it is true or believes it is true. A hypothesis explains a fact, but it is also itself a statement of fact, that is, a statement that is either true or false depending upon the way things are. For example, if you believe that the wind blew your homework off your desk, but your cat was really to blame, then the wind hypothesis is mistaken. No amount of believing the wind hypothesis will change the fact that your cat was really responsible. For this reason, articles that offer a hypothesis must present evidence to support the hypothesis. They cannot rely just upon preference or personal opinion.

To evaluate the articles in this book critically, let us begin by considering which authors offer hypotheses—statements of fact that can be used to explain other facts. Not all of the authors in this book necessarily offer their own hypothesis. Some of the articles are concerned with critiquing a hypothesis offered by an author on the opposing side. We can consider such articles to be offering a negative hypothesis, that is, the hypothesis that the correct explanation is something other than the hypothesis offered by the opposing side. Still other articles offer neither a hypothesis nor a negative hypothesis but a discussion on the nature of evidence and hypothetical reasoning as it pertains to this topic. In those cases, we will have to be content to state the thesis, or

Author	Hypothesis
William Paley	
Harold S. Slusher	The presence of certain isotopes in rocks was caused by something other than long-term, regular radioactive decay.
John C. Whitcomb and Henry M. Morris	
Duane T. Gish	The complexity of life on Earth was caused by something other than evolution through natural selection.
Phillip E. Johnson	The origin of life on Earth was caused by something other than the spontaneous appearance of a self-replicating process.
William A. Dembski	Patterns can be analyzed mathematically for evidence of intelligent design.
William Jennings Bryan	The immorality of modern times is being caused by belief in evolution.
Charles Darwin	The complexity of life on Earth was caused by evolution through natural selection.
Tim M. Berra	The presence of certain isotopes in rocks was caused by long-term, regular radioactive decay.
Chris McGowan	The extinction of some species (and the survival of others) was caused by something other than a worldwide flood.
Philip Kitcher	
Michael Ruse	It is too much to expect a single observation to verify or falsify any hypothesis.
Richard Dawkins	The origin of life on Earth was caused by the spontaneous appearance of a self-replicating process.
James Rachels	

main point of the article, rather than a hypothesis.

In the table on page 170, you can recognize which articles offer a hypothesis by looking for the words *caused by*. You can recognize articles that offer a negative hypothesis by looking for the additional words *something other than*. However, four lines have been left empty. See if you can identify the main point of the article and state it in the form of a hypothesis, a negative hypothesis, or (if it is just a discussion of hypothetical reasoning) a thesis.

Since a hypothesis is an explanation for an observed fact, the fact that it attempts to explain should be as concrete and clear as possible. Look at the seventh hypothesis in the table above: "The immorality of modern times is being caused by belief in evolution." The concept *immorality* is difficult to define and observe, since different people have quite different opinions on which actions might be considered immoral. It would be better to make this hypothesis more specific. Bryan's article mentions three specific types of immorality, namely, an attitude that it is best not to care for the weak and helpless, an approval of sexual promiscuity, and an increased use of scientific technology in war. Most of his arguments focus on the first of these. So a better hypothesis would be this:

William Jennings Bryan	The modern attitude that it is best not to care for the weak and helpless is caused by belief in evolution.

Are there any other hypotheses in the above table that you could make more specific?

Note that not every article offers a hypothesis, even a negative hypothesis. Hence, we cannot use hypothetical reasoning to evaluate all of the articles. For example, look at the "hypothesis" stated in the table for the article by William A. Dembski: "Patterns can be analyzed mathematically for evidence of intelligent design." This statement does not offer an explanation for specific patterns. All it states is that patterns caused by intelligent design and patterns that occur randomly have different mathematical properties. If this claim is true, we can use the mathematical properties of a pattern to test whether it was caused by an intelligent designer (such as God), or occurred accidentally. Dembski is not proposing a hypothesis; he is proposing a way to test hypotheses. Since a good hypothesis must be testable, Dembski is proposing a way to test the hypothesis that the complexity of life on Earth was caused by God. We cannot use hypothetical reasoning to evaluate this claim, but it is important to keep Dembski's argument in mind when evaluating the testability of claims made by other authors. Similarly, the claim made by Michael Ruse is not a hypothesis. It is a claim about the relationship between hypotheses and observations that will presumably help us understand how to evaluate hypotheses offered by other authors.

2. Gather the author's evidence supporting the hypothesis.

Once you have a hypothesis, you must gather the evidence the author uses to support that hypothesis. Sometimes this evidence can be expressed in a single sentence, but usually the author will use several sentences, or even several paragraphs, to describe and explain the evidence that he or she claims supports his or her hypothesis. Let's look at the second article in chapter one to see what kind of evidence Harold S. Slusher uses to support his claim that the presence of certain isotopes (chemicals with a specific atomic weight) in rocks is due to something other than long-term, regular radioactive decay. This is a good article to use as an example, since readers who are not familiar with chemistry may need some help with its highly technical arguments. The following list presents some of Slusher's evidence:

1. The half-life of radioactive materials (the time it takes

for half of a quantity of radioactive material to decay) has not been determined with sufficient accuracy.

2. Radioactive decay is not regular, since
   a. radioactive decay may be affected by cosmic rays (radiation from space), which may not always be striking the earth with the same intensity;
   b. observations of "pleochroic haloes," which should measure the regularity of radioactive decay, indicate a lack of regularity.
3. Assumptions about the amount of isotope in a rock when it was first formed are just guesses.
4. The amount of an isotope in a rock may be affected by various processes that "have nothing to do with radioactive decay," such as
   a. changes in the quantity of those isotopes on Earth due to meteors and meteorites;
   b. leaching of isotopes out of rocks by ground water.

3. Evaluate the evidence.

There are some specific criteria that scientists use in evaluating hypotheses. The first of these is that a good hypothesis explains many facts and, ideally, a wide variety of facts. For example, the wind hypothesis to explain why your homework is on the floor may also explain why only light objects are on the floor and why the room is so chilly. The cat could have knocked off heavier objects, and it would have done so without affecting the temperature of the room.

Because the number and variety of facts is so important to a scientific hypothesis, it is important to assess these facts carefully. When reading an article, it is easy to assume that everything an author says is really true. This is particularly easy to do when the subject under discussion is highly technical, as in the case of Slusher's article. However, let's look at the facts that Slusher offers us to see if we can determine how reliable they actually are. Sometimes authors expect us to take their word for certain facts. Other times they support the facts by citing someone else, either an eyewitness or an expert, to vouch for the facts. Given the nature of this discussion, Slusher does not appeal to eyewitnesses. After all, no one can live long enough to witness the passage of geological time, even if Slusher is right that the earth is only a few thousand years old. However, Slusher does frequently cite experts to vouch for the facts he offers.

Expert testimony (items 1, 2a, and 2b). No scientist can perform every experiment or make every observation firsthand. For this reason, scientists depend upon careful reports of experiments and observations done by other scientists. Expert testimony is an important element of any scientific argument. However, relying upon the testimony of others can become a bad habit. Advertisers love to exploit this habit to sell their products. Commercials for pain relievers often feature actors dressed as doctors in an attempt to convince us that the product being sold is endorsed by "scientists." In some commercials, the "expert" who endorses the product has no credentials other than being famous and well liked. To assess the reliability of a fact supported by expert testimony, we need to ask two questions. First, is the expert cited really an expert, that is, really qualified to vouch for the facts in question? Second, does the expert really say what the author claims he or she says?

In support of claim 2a that cosmic rays vary in the intensity with which they strike the earth, Slusher cites work done by Dr. T.G. Barnes. Is Barnes qualified? In fact, Barnes is not considered to be an expert in this field by most other scientists. By doing a little Internet research, you can discover that Barnes earned a master's degree in physics from Brown University (a large and respected institution), but his doctorate is merely an honorary degree awarded by a college particularly sympathetic to his views. Barnes's work may or may not be valid on its own merits, but in this context his testimony as an expert is not particularly convincing. In support of claims 1 and 2b, Slusher offers the testimony of scientists who are genuinely experts. (Look them up on the Internet to verify that this is true.) Hence, Slusher's claims here are more convincing. However, it is still worth checking to see what these experts are really saying. Physicist G.H. Henderson, for example, is not saying that his measurements of pleochroic haloes indicate that the rate of radioactive decay has been irregular. He is saying that the variability of his measurements indicate that "other factors" intervened to destroy the accuracy of his measurements—something that happens all too frequently in scientific experiments.

Unsupported statements of fact (items 3, 4a, and 4b). Statements of fact do not need to be supported by testimony when they are sufficiently widely accepted to be considered common knowledge. Common knowledge does not necessarily mean that everyone can be expected to know it. Rather, a fact is considered common knowledge when so many experts have vouched for the fact that it is impractical to cite them all. Should items 3, 4a, and 4b be considered common knowledge? To find out for sure, it would be necessary to do some research to discover whether these facts really are widely accepted within the scientific community. It is precisely because such research can be difficult that it is tempting simply to take the author's word for it. Regrettably, critical thinking does require some effort. Making up your mind in a vacuum, without doing the requisite checking, is not what is meant by *critical thinking*.

Often, checking on the extent to which a fact is considered common knowledge will not yield an unambiguous answer. Many facts stated by an author can be partly true and partly false. Slusher's claims 3, 4a, and 4b are good examples. Any scientist would certainly admit Slusher's claim 3, that the amount of isotope in a rock when it was first formed is just a guess. However, most scientists think that it is a guess based on well-justified assumptions, that is, that it is a *good* guess. Likewise, any scientist would admit claims 4a and 4b, that various processes may alter the amount of a particular isotope in a rock, making radiometric measurements on that particular rock invalid. But most scientists do not believe that this happens to all rocks, and they believe they can tell which rocks yield valid measurements and which do not. Hence, Slusher's common knowledge claims should not be considered particularly convincing, but they should also not be dismissed as simply false.

Aside from the reliability of the facts offered in support of a hypothesis, two other criteria generally enter into hypothetical reasoning. One of these is the simplicity and plausibility of the hypothesis. The other is the testability of the hypothesis. Let's briefly consider these criteria as they apply to Slusher's article.

When considering a hypothesis, simplicity and plausibility go together. Generally speaking, the simpler a hypothesis is, the more believable it is. This principle is often referred to as Ockham's Razor in honor of the medieval philosopher, William of Ockham, who first developed this principle of hypothetical reasoning. The hypothesis that the wind blew your homework off your desk, for example, is quite simple and believable. It does not require the action of extra mysterious forces. Everyone is familiar with wind and its effects. It does not appeal to the action of lots of agents, nor does it require complex planning on the part of those agents. It does not appeal to unusual circumstances or coincidences (unless, of course, you rarely leave your window open). Because the hypothesis is relatively simple and elegant, we find it easy to believe. By contrast, the polter-geist theory requires the operation of mysterious forces. The cat theory does not require mysterious forces, but it may be more complex since it requires someone (an agent) to let the cat into your room and then let it out again. Because these hypotheses are more complex, they are also more dif-ficult to believe, although this does not prove they are false.

Slusher's hypothesis is naturally fairly complex. This is to be expected, since Slusher is proposing a negative hypothe-sis. He is arguing that the amount of certain isotopes in rocks is not due primarily to radioactive decay but to some-thing else, that is, to various factors, including isotopes brought to earth by meteors and meteorites, leaching of iso-topes by ground water, and so forth. Thus, he appeals to many mechanisms instead of only one. However, he does not appeal to mysterious forces, complex planning by one or more agents, or unusual circumstances or coincidences.

The final criterion for judging a hypothesis is testability. Testability often involves practical considerations. How could you test whether or not the wind was responsible for blowing your homework onto the floor? You might put your homework back on your desk, then hold an electric fan near the window to see if air blowing from that direc-tion is capable of disturbing your homework. However, this test requires that you have an electric fan and know how to use it. It is often difficult to say how testable a hypothesis is, since the only way to show that a hypothesis is testable is to think of a practical way to test it. Some tests, unfortunately, require the right kind of scientific equipment and the knowledge to use it.

How testable is Slusher's hypothesis? It is difficult to say. Much of the point of Slusher's article is to draw into ques-tion the very tests that might ordinarily be used to check a hypothesis about radioactive decay.

4. Consider alternative hypotheses (explanations for the evidence).

As you consider the evidence that an author presents for his or her hypothesis, you should keep in mind the alternative explanations that might be expected to fit the facts. Some authors will do a good job of presenting these alternatives, but other authors will not. If the author considers only one explanation for the evidence, he or she may be presenting a biased, or one-sided, view or may not have fully considered the issue.

As it happens, Slusher does a careful job of presenting and explaining the alternative to his hypothesis. In fact, since his hypothesis is the negative hypothesis that something else is responsible for the quantities of isotopes found in rocks other than long-term, regular radioactive decay, it is necessary for him to explain the alternative hypothesis so readers can understand what his something else is opposed to.

5. Draw a conclusion about the author's hypothesis.

Finally, after considering the evidence and alternative explanations, it is time to make a judgment, to decide whether the hypothesis makes sense. You can tally up the evidence that does or does not support the hypothesis and see how many pros and cons you have. But critical thinking is more complex than just keeping score. Some evidence deserves to be given more weight than others. For example, the controversy over pleochroic haloes is much more important to Slusher's argument than the question of the margin of error in laboratory measurements of atomic half-life. You have to decide how much the success or failure on these questions should affect your judgment of his argument as a whole. What do you think—does Slusher adequately support the hypothesis that something other than long-term, regular radioactive decay is the primary factor responsible for the amount of certain isotopes in rocks?

Exploring Further

Let's examine another article using hypothetical reasoning. Read Richard Dawkins's article. Once you have read the article, you might start your evaluation by learning something about Richard Dawkins himself, beginning with the brief note provided by the editor. If necessary, do some additional research to discover whether Dawkins has an advanced degree in the field he is writing about, whether he holds an academic appointment at a respected university, and whether he has written other books on this subject. Are his opinions widely respected in the scientific community?

Now let's review Dawkins's article using the five steps for hypothetical reasoning.

1. State a hypothesis.

The origin of life on Earth was caused by the spontaneous appearance of a self-replicating process.

2. Gather the author's evidence.
    1. In developing a theory of the origin of life, we are entitled to assume quite a bit of "luck" because
        a. the probability of any event occurring depends upon the number of chances available for it to occur;
        b. there are "many planets in the universe where life *could* have originated."
    2. Crystals found in clays and muds are capable of replicating.
    3. Variant forms of crystals may be better at replicating than other forms.
    4. Organic (carbon-based) molecules in particular are known to affect the "flow of fluids" and the breakup and growth of crystals.
    5. There is a close chemical association of organic mol-

ecules and inorganic clay crystals.

6. Self-replicating clay crystals no longer present on Earth could have given rise to self-replicating organic molecules.

3. Evaluate the evidence.

Unlike living organisms, most of the objects around us do not have the ability to make copies of themselves. Chairs cannot; pens cannot. Even very complicated machines such as computers cannot. Engineers can design machines that are capable of making copies of themselves, but this is not easy to do, and it is impossible to imagine that such machines could fall together by accident. It is reasonable to suppose that the mere ability to replicate is so complex that an entity with this ability could not have arisen without the help of an intelligent designer.

Obviously, the spontaneous origin of a self-replicating process is a highly improbable event. Hence, Dawkins's argument must do two things. On the one hand, it must show that the amount of improbability (or luck) that we can tolerate in an acceptable theory is quite high. On the other hand, it must show that a replicating mechanism capable of giving rise to modern life is simple enough that it could have occurred by accident, given the amount of luck we are allowed to assume. How well do the facts offered by Dawkins accomplish these two goals?

Unsupported statements of fact (items 1a and 1b). Dawkins does not cite expert or eyewitness testimony in support of claims 1a and 1b. Apparently, he assumes that these are items of common knowledge. Are they? The first claim is a statement about probability theory. The probability that an event will occur some time or other depends upon how many chances (or trials) there will be. For example, you would not want to bet your life that a single roll of a die will come up six, but you would be quite safe to bet your life that a six will come up at least once in a hundred rolls. You have probably had enough experience with dice to vouch for this claim yourself. It is clearly an instance of common knowledge. The second claim is more difficult. Is it common knowledge that there are many planets in the universe on which life could have originated (but perhaps did not)?

Expert testimony (items 2, 3, 4, 5, and 6). In this article, Dawkins is summarizing a hypothesis explained in much greater detail by another scientist, chemist Graham Cairns-Smith. However, Dawkins himself remarks that Cairns-Smith's hypothesis is a "less-fashionable theory" than the primeval soup theories under which organic molecules are thought to begin replicating spontaneously without any scaffolding provided by replicating clay crystals. Does Dawkins weaken his case by using a less fashionable theory? Are scientists other than Cairns-Smith willing to vouch for the facts that Dawkins presents?

Once you have considered the reliability of the facts presented, you should apply the other criteria for assessing hypothetical reasoning: simplicity (plausibility) and testability. Dawkins's hypothesis does not require the action of mysterious forces. It depends primarily on the known laws of probability and known chemical properties of silicate crystals and carbon molecules. It does not appeal to the action of conscious agents or to complex planning. However, it does appeal to coincidence and special circumstances. The spontaneous emergence of replicating clay crystals is an event that must occur just by accident, according to this theory. Of course, Dawkins is aware of this weakness in his hypothesis, which is why he is so concerned to argue that we can tolerate a great deal of luck, or coincidence, in a theory of this sort. On balance, what do you think? Does Dawkins offer a sufficiently simple and believable hypothesis? Finally, can you think of any way that Dawkins's hypothesis might be tested? What sorts of equipment and knowledge would you need in order to perform a test?

4. Consider alternative hypotheses.

The alternative to Dawkins's hypothesis that life began spontaneously is that life was started by an intelligent designer, namely, God. In the brief passage presented in this book, Dawkins does not consider this alternative (although he does consider it elsewhere in the book from which the passage was taken). How does the alternative hypothesis compare to Dawkins's hypothesis? Once again, we can apply the criteria of simplicity (plausibility) and testability. Unlike Dawkins's hypothesis, the hypothesis that life was created by God does not appeal to coincidence, so it is much simpler in that regard. Some people might consider God to be a "mysterious force," but this judgment may be unfair. Many more people believe in God than in, say, poltergeists. The chief weakness of the alternative hypothesis is that it appeals to complex planning by a conscious agent (namely, God). Now, everyone knows that some events are the result of complex planning by conscious agents, so the fact that a hypothesis appeals to such an agent does not mean it is false. However, in general, good hypotheses try to avoid appeals to conscious agents where possible. Given that the alternative hypothesis is simpler in some respects, but more complex in other respects, which hypothesis do you think is simpler and more believable on balance? Can you think of any way to test the alternative hypothesis? What sorts of equipment and knowledge would you need?

5. Draw a conclusion.

You decide: Taking the reliability of the facts, the simplicity of the hypothesis (and its alternative), and the testability of the hypothesis (and its alternative) into account, does Dawkins make a good case for his hypothesis concerning the origin of life? Which considerations most influence your decision?

Now You Do It!

Choose an article from this book that has not already been analyzed and use hypothetical reasoning to determine if the author's evidence supports the hypothesis. Here is a form you can use:

Name of article_____ Author_____

1. State the author's hypothesis.

2. List the evidence.

3. Examine the evidence. For each item you have listed under number 2, state whether the evidence is unsupported or supported by expert or eyewitness testimony. Are the unsupported statements generally accepted as common knowledge? Are the experts or eyewitnesses regarded as reliable? Do they really say what the author claims they say? Is the author's hypothesis simple (plausible) and testable?

4. Consider alternative hypotheses. What alternative hypotheses might be proposed, and does the author consider them? How do the alternative hypotheses compare in terms of simplicity (plausibility) and testability to the author's hypothesis?

5. Draw a conclusion. Does the author adequately support his or her claim? Do you believe the author's hypothesis is better than the alternative? Explain.

For Further Research

Tim M. Berra, *Evolution and the Myth of Creationism: A Basic Guide to the Facts in the Evolution Debate.* Stanford, CA: Stanford University Press, 1990.

I.L. Cohen, *Darwin Was Wrong: A Study in Probabilities.* Greenvale, NY: New Research Publications, 1984.

Charles Darwin, *The Origin of Species by Means of Natural Selection, or the Preservation of Favored Races in the Struggle for Life.* 1859. Reprint, Baltimore: Penguin Books, 1968.

Richard Dawkins, *The Blind Watchmaker: Why the Evidence of Evolution Reveals a Universe Without Design.* New York: Norton, 1986.

——, *The Selfish Gene.* New York: Oxford University Press, 1990.

William A. Dembski, *No Free Lunch: Why Specified Complexity Cannot Be Purchased Without Intelligence.* Lanham, MD: Rowman & Littlefield, 2002.

Daniel Dennett, *Darwin's Dangerous Idea: Evolution and the Meaning of Life.* New York: Simon and Schuster, 1995.

Robert J. Dunzweiler, *A Proposed Creationist Alternative to Evolutionism.* Hatfield, PA: Interdisciplinary Biblical Research Institute, 1983.

Niles Eldridge, *The Triumph of Evolution, and the Failure of Creationism.* New York: W.H. Freeman, 2000.

Raymond A. Eve and Francis B. Harrold, *The Creationist Movement in Modern America.* Boston: Twayne, 1990.

Wayne Friar, *A Case for Creation*. Chicago: Moody Press, 1983.

Roland Mushat Frye, ed., *Is God a Creationist? The Religious Case Against Creation-Science*. New York: Scribner's, 1983.

Duane T. Gish, *Creation Scientists Answer Their Critics*. El Cajon, CA: Institute for Creation Research, 1993.

———, *Evolution: The Fossils Say No!* San Diego, CA: Creation-Life, 1978.

———, *Evolution: The Fossils Still Say No!* El Cajon, CA: Institute for Creation Research, 1995.

Stephen Jay Gould, "Evolution as Fact and Theory," *Hen's Teeth and Horse's Toes*. New York: W.W. Norton, 1983.

Melvin L. Greenhut and John G. Greenhut, *Science and God: Our Amazing Physical and Economic Universe, Accidental or God Created?* Lanham, MD: University Press of America, 2002.

Francis B. Harrold and Raymond A. Eve, eds., *Cult Archaeology and Creationism: Understanding Pseudoscientific Beliefs About the Past*. Iowa City: University of Iowa Press, 1987.

Institute of Creation Research, *Scientific Creationism* (Public School Edition). Ed. Henry M. Morris. San Diego, CA: Creation-Life, 1981.

Phillip E. Johnson, *The Creation Hypothesis: Scientific Evidence for an Intelligent Designer*. Downers Grove, IL: InterVarsity Press, 1994.

———, *Darwin on Trial*. Downers Grove, IL: InterVarsity Press, 1993.

Philip Kitcher, *Abusing Science: The Case Against Creationism*. Cambridge, MA: MIT Press, 1990.

Lester P. Lane, and Raymond G. Bohlin, *The Natural Limits to Biological Change*. Grand Rapids, MI: Zondervan, 1984.

Chris McGowan, *In the Beginning . . . A Scientist Shows Why the Creationists Are Wrong*. Amherst, NY: Prometheus Books, 1984.

John A. Moore, *From Genesis to Genetics: The Case of Evolution and Creationism*. Berkeley: University of California Press, 2002.

J.P. Moreland and John Mark Reynolds, eds., *Three Views on Creation and Evolution*. Grand Rapids, MI: Zondervan, 1999.

Henry M. Morris, *Biblical Creationism: What Each Book of the Bible Teaches About Creation and the Flood*. Grand Rapids, MI: Baker Books, 1993.

——, *The Long War Against God: The History and Impact of the Creation/Evolution Conflict*. Grand Rapids, MI: Baker Book House, 1989.

Henry M. Morris and Gary E. Parker, *What Is Creation Science?* El Cajon, CA: Master Books, 1987.

Ronald L. Numbers, *The Creationists*. New York: Knopf, 1992.

William Paley, *Natural Theology: Evidences of the Existence and Attributes of the Deity*. Philadelphia: Printed for John Morgan by H. Maxwell, 1802.

Robert T. Pennock, *Tower of Babel: The Evidence Against the New Creationism*. Cambridge, MA: MIT Press, 1999.

Robert T. Pennock, ed. *Intelligent Design Creationism and Its Critics: Philosophical, Theological, and Scientific Perspectives*. Cambridge, MA: MIT Press, 2001.

Mossimo Pigliucci, *Denying Evolution: Creationism, Scientism, and the Nature of Science*. Sunderland, MA: Sinauer Associates, 2002.

Ian Plimer, *Telling Lies for God: Reason vs. Creationism.* Milson's Point, New South Wales: Random House Australia, 1994.

James Rachels, *Created from Animals: The Moral Implications of Darwinism.* New York: Oxford University Press, 1990.

Del Ratzsch, *The Battle of Beginnings: Why Neither Side Is Winning the Creation-Evolution Debate.* Downers Grove, IL: InterVarsity Press, 1996.

Michael Ruse, *Darwinism Defended: A Guide to the Evolution Controversies.* Menlo Park, CA: Benjamin/Cummings, 1982.

Harold S. Slusher, *Critique of Radiometric Dating.* San Diego, CA: Creation-Life, 1973.

Elliott Sober, *Philosophy of Biology.* Boulder, CO: Westview Press, 1993.

Arthur N. Strahler, *Science and Earth History: The Evolution/ Creation Controversy.* Buffalo, NY: Prometheus Books, 1999.

Adell Thompson, *Biology, Zoology, and Genetics: Evolution Model vs. Creation Model.* Washington, DC: University Press of America, 1983.

Lee Tiffin, *Creationism's Upside-Down Pyramid: How Science Refutes Fundamentalism.* Amherst, NY: Prometheus Books, 1994.

Alfred Russel Wallace, *An Anthology of His Shorter Writings.* Ed. Charles H. Smith. New York: Oxford University Press, 1991.

John C. Whitcomb, *The Early Earth: An Introduction to Biblical Creationism.* Grand Rapids, MI: Baker Book House, 1986.

John C. Whitcomb and Henry M. Morris, *The Genesis Flood: The Biblical Record and Its Scientific Implications.* Nutley, NJ: Presbyterian and Reform Publishing, 1961.

Daniel E. Wonderly, *Neglect of Geological Data: Sedimentary Strata Compared with Young-Earth Creationist Writings.* Hatfield, PA: Interdisciplinary Biblical Research Institute, 1987.

Willard Young, *Fallacies of Creationism.* Calgary, Canada: Detselig Enterprises, 1985.

Index